# BALD KNOBBERS

## CHRONICLES OF VIGILANTE JUSTICE

VINCENT S. ANDERSON

Published by The History Press
Charleston, SC 29403
www.historypress.net

Copyright © 2013 by Vincent S. Anderson
All rights reserved

*Front cover, bottom*: "Before the Drop," circa 1896. D.S. Cole, Carrolton, Missouri. *Library of Congress Prints and Photographs Division, Washington, D.C., LC-USZ62-79432.*

First published 2013

Manufactured in the United States

ISBN 978.1.62619.201.0

Library of Congress CIP data applied for.

*Notice*: The information in this book is true and complete to the best of our knowledge. It is offered without guarantee on the part of the author or The History Press. The author and The History Press disclaim all liability in connection with the use of this book.

All rights reserved. No part of this book may be reproduced or transmitted in any form whatsoever without prior written permission from the publisher except in the case of brief quotations embodied in critical articles and reviews.

# CONTENTS

Dedication                                                              5
Introduction                                                            9

PART I: TANEY COUNTY
1. The Origin of the Bald Knobber Idea                                 13
2. The Murder of J.M. Everett                                          17
3. Organized as a Secret Society                                       20
4. The Knobbers Begin Work Mildly                                      25
5. The Knobbers' First Lynching                                        27
6. Taney Court House Burned                                            34
7. No-Account Killing of Buck Mercer                                   36
8. Andrew Coggburn: Shot to Death by the Knobber Chief                 37
9. The Anti-Baldknobber Militia                                        42
10. Murdered for Money to Get Married With                             45
11. Sam Snapp: Murdered by a Bald Knobber                              47
12. Reuben Pruitt: Shot Dead by a Bald Knobber                         49
13. A Duel in the Scrub Oaks                                           50
14. A Bald Knobber Romance                                             52
15. Knobber Chiefton Dies—With His Boots On                            57
16. Split in the Order of Pistols                                      61
17. Difficulty in Getting a Sheriff                                    65
18. Trials & Acquittals                                                67
19. A Boy Who Died Rather Than Suffer Dishonor                         69
20. Knobber Wife Insane: An Awful Tragedy                              71

# Contents

**PART II: CHRISTIAN COUNTY**

| | |
|---|---|
| 1. Convicted by His Ass | 75 |
| 2. Whipped Before He Was Murdered | 80 |
| 3. The Murder of Edens and Green | 83 |
| 4. The Civil Authorities Interested at Last | 86 |
| 5. Joe Inman Confesses: Shot Down Out of Sport | 89 |
| 6. Mathews Confesses to the Butchery | 94 |
| 7. Rev. C.O. Simmons: Grieved in Spirit | 96 |
| 8. Lured by His Sweetheart | 99 |
| 9. Charlie Graves Makes a Clean Breast | 101 |
| 10. The Blessings of Liberty—From Jail | 105 |
| 11. Bald Knobber Prisoners & Crazed Wife | 107 |
| 12. Trial of Gilbert Applegate | 113 |
| 13. Applegate Acquitted | 122 |
| 14. Quintuple Lynching | 124 |
| 15. How the Matter Stands: December 18th, 1888 | 126 |
| 16. Set Free by Friends | 130 |
| 17. Prisoners at Large & Starved | 132 |
| 18. Bungling Work of an Execution | 134 |
| 19. A Knobber Melodrama | 139 |
| 20. Knobbers and the Anti: Waging War | 140 |
| 21. The Bald Knobbers Reign | 143 |
| 22. Murder of Mrs. John Wesley Bright | 147 |
| 23. Accomplice Betrays Secrets | 150 |
| 24. Tragedy Ends in a Farce | 153 |

**PART III: LIFE IN THE OZARKS**

| | |
|---|---|
| 1. A Bald Knobber's Cabin | 157 |
| 2. Plucky Woman Saved Her Husband | 167 |
| 3. Knobber Wives Refuse Discouragement | 169 |
| 4. Meet Sarah Walker | 171 |

| | |
|---|---|
| Conclusion: I'd Been Born Again | 173 |
| Appendix: The Ballad of the Bald Knobbers | 175 |
| Bibliography | 179 |
| Index | 185 |
| About the Author | 191 |

# DEDICATION

As a young boy growing up in Ozark County, Missouri, I had always heard the saga of the notorious Bald Knobbers. These Ozark vigilantes have become a part of Ozark folklore, and they have always held my fascination. I remember seeing them represented by manikins at *Silver Dollar City* near Branson, Missouri, and scenes of them were painted on the walls at the Fire in the Hole ride. The Bald Knobbers also make their nightly raid and set a cabin on fire in the outdoor drama *The Shepherd of the Hills*.

When I was a child, my favorite singing group was the *Baldknobbers Hillbilly Jamboree Stage Show* from Branson, Missouri. George Aggernite (Lyle W. Mabe) was one of the main characters I always watched on stage because, in my mind, he was larger than life. Every so often, he would also appear on the nightly ten o'clock Channel 3 News, KYTV, out of Springfield, Missouri. George would crack a few jokes or ad-lib to somebody, while doing a commercial for Empire Gas before the weather forecast. I didn't get to watch him often because we didn't have a TV—we lived too far in the valley to get a signal. Sometimes, I would spend the night at my grandmother's home because she had a TV, and I knew she would watch the ten o'clock news. Consequently, I would see George Aggernite with his toothless smile.

I also remember the *Baldknobbers Hillbilly Jamboree Stage Show* traveling to nearby Mountain Home, Arkansas, in late April 1972 for a performance. Ticket prices were $1.25 for adults and $0.50 for children. This jamboree consisted of some wild characters and great musicians, such as the Wild Man on the guitar, Droopy Drawers playing the washboard and George

# Dedication

*Baldknobber Hillbilly Jamboree Stage Show*, 1972. *Author's collection.*

# Dedication

Aggernite thumping a string on a washtub. The small school stage was packed full of musicians and equipment, and the night began in the gym auditorium with enormous excitement. After the second song, comedian George Aggernite was announced. As he ran onto the stage, he tripped over his washtub and fell off the platform. A collective moan could be heard across the auditorium. George Aggernite was the consummate entertainer and performer; he crawled back on the stage, cracked a few jokes, played a song and then went backstage to bandage his cut leg. He came back a few moments later and acted like nothing was wrong.

After reading the articles in this book, one might see the term Bald Knobber as a name that is despised and unredeemable. The initial vigilante leader of the Bald Knobbers was a man named Captain Nathaniel N. Kinney, whose nickname was the "Old Blue Gobbler." It is with him that the lore of the Bald Knobbers began. Nevertheless, this book is dedicated to the memory of George Aggernite, a different kind of Baldknobber, who brought smiles and laughter to the Ozark hills, where there had been dissention, poverty and tears.

Thanks, Mr. Aggernite.

# INTRODUCTION

In the past, the Ozarks had a few regional political parties of their own, though we haven't seen them on the ballot lately. The two parties I'm referring to are the Bald Knobbers and the Anti-Bald Knobbers. To the defense of the Bald Knobbers, it all started out with good intentions: the determination of freedom to practice their religion and morals. As we look at these historical characters, not only will we discover the prejudice and terror once endured, but we may also discover the darker side of our natures. These events spanned mostly Taney and Christian Counties in Missouri. Yet the surrounding Ozark region and counties also had divided hearts concerning the issues of that time.

One book chronicling these Ozark desperadoes is called *Bald Knobbers: Vigilantes on the Ozarks Frontier* by Elmo Ingenthron and Mary Hartman. According to these authors, the Bald Knobbers were mostly Republicans and former Unionists, while the Anti-Bald Knobbers were mostly Democrats and former Confederate soldiers.

Over the past five years, I have read and compiled over six hundred old newspaper articles concerning the Bald Knobbers. Many were repeated in similar wording and fashion. During my research, I have distilled the Bald Knobber saga into forty-nine chapters. Many chapters are a compilation of two to five articles. The purpose of this book is to present the original newspaper articles that covered the 1880s' and '90s' perspectives of the Bald Knobbers. Additionally, these stories are for the readers to glean for themselves the facts as people from that era did.

# INTRODUCTION

These stories contain interviews, letters, confessions and testimonies of many of the main characters of the region. Additionally, some biographical details and genealogical information of prominent Bald Knobbers are furnished. The crimes and punishments are documented in graphic detail. I have endeavored to maintain the integrity of the original letters written by Bald Knobbers, including the nineteenth-century spelling and the unique newsprint format concurrent with the 1880s and '90s. Furthermore, these chapters contain a record of everyday life in the Ozarks, including the local Ozark vernacular and euphuisms. These stories also document the prejudice from the North and its perceptions of hillbilly ignorance in southern states.

I have endeavored to compile, transcribe and edit these news articles in the historical essence and flavor in which they were originally written. Though some stories and lines contain the bias of that era, I have not deleted or edited them. These articles are not all inclusive, but they provide snapshots that are a part of our Ozarks history.

VINCENT S. ANDERSON

*Part I*

# TANEY COUNTY

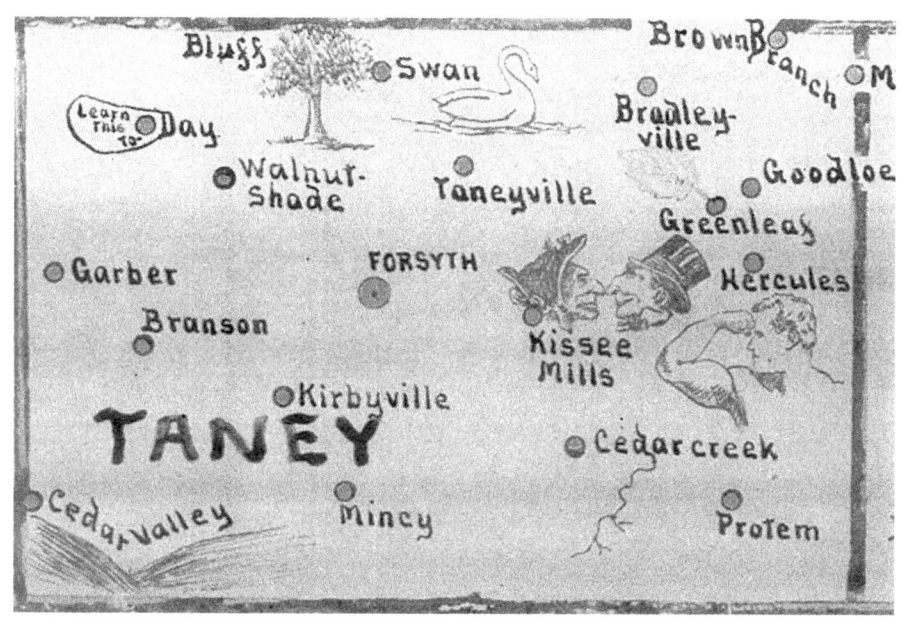

Galbraith's Railway Mail Service Maps, Taney County, Missouri, 1898. *Library of Congress.*

# 1
# THE ORIGIN OF THE BALD KNOBBER IDEA

The Bald Knob Society originated in Taney [pronounced Tawney] county. In the language of Parson Dennison, an opponent, it was "a beam-eyed society for the eradication of notes." The man who conceived the idea and became the Grand Chief of the order was Capt. N.N. Kinney. He lived on a ranch near Forsyth, the county seat. Kinney was a remarkable man in several respects. He was 6 feet 6 inches tall, but was so well proportioned that no one would have thought him so tall unless he were standing by an ordinary six-footer.

He weighed 290 pounds ordinarily. He had a big head with plenty of active brains. He was black haired and black eyed, and as handsome as [he] was big. He had been a Captain in the Union army and a special frontier agent of the Post Office Department, where he is said to have killed several men who at one time [or] another resisted arrest for holding up stages. Finally he came to Springfield where he opened a saloon. It is said to have been a very popular saloon. With the money he made in selling liquor he bought a square mile of land down in Taney county and stocked it with cattle, sheep, and hogs, and there lived the life of a ranchman. He was about 48 years old when he went to Taney county. He had two children, a boy and a girl, both young, and a stepson, J.A. DeLong, who is now editor of the *Taney County News* and Prosecuting Attorney of the county. Capt. Kinney did not find society in Taney county exactly to his liking.

In a formal statement concerning the origin of the Bald Knobbers made a short time before he was shot to death Kinney said:

*So far as I could learn, the history of Taney county had been a record of lawlessness and disregard of social proprieties. When I came here some four years ago* [1883] *it was common for men to live with women to whom they had never been married. Why, one old Mormon-like neighbor kept six women. Then the county was $42,000 in debt and had not even a plank to show for it. The money had simply vanished, over thirty men had been shot to death in the county since the war, and not one of the murderers had been punished by the civil authorities. Well, I had come here to lead a retired and quiet life, but I could not refrain from expressing my opinions of such things, and I cannot refrain now. The consequence was that men came to me and said: "Kinney, you had better look out. These people don't like your talk, and you better go slow or you will get it in the neck."*

*Well, I have had some experience in this line myself, and I say these things should be condemned, and I propose to condemn them. The best men in the county gradually drifted to my side, and it became a war between civilization and barbarism.*

That people were grossly immoral, that the county had been robbed, and that many deliberate murders—the number is estimated all the way from thirty-two to forty-two—had been committed and no one punished for them even by imprisonment, are undisputed facts. It is a matter of record that when in 1883 two professional burglars from St. Louis drilled down through Taney county and robbed the county treasury at Forsyth of $3,000 [they] were afterward convicted and sentenced to the penitentiary for two years each. No man had been sentenced to the penitentiary from Taney county in twenty years before on any account. When Capt. Kinney talked in public about those things the county officials retorted that he was not, as an ex-saloon keeper from the slums of Springfield, a proper censor of Taney county morals. People gradually took sides with either Kinney or the officials. Among these officials were Thomas A. Layton, County Clerk; Sampson Barker, County Clerk; John Moseley, Sheriff; and T.C. Spellings, Prosecuting Attorney. The Bald Knobbers of Taney county say that Spellings was simply weak, and permitted criminals to go unpunished because the gang that elected him and held the other offices made him do it.

As the broach widened, Capt. Kinney, from his experience on the frontier, saw the necessity of organization if he was to live in the county in security. His friends say that he wanted an organization to preserve order and enforce the civil law. His enemies say that he wanted a gang under him for his own aggrandizement, and incidentally for his own safety. Every man owned arms of some sort, and

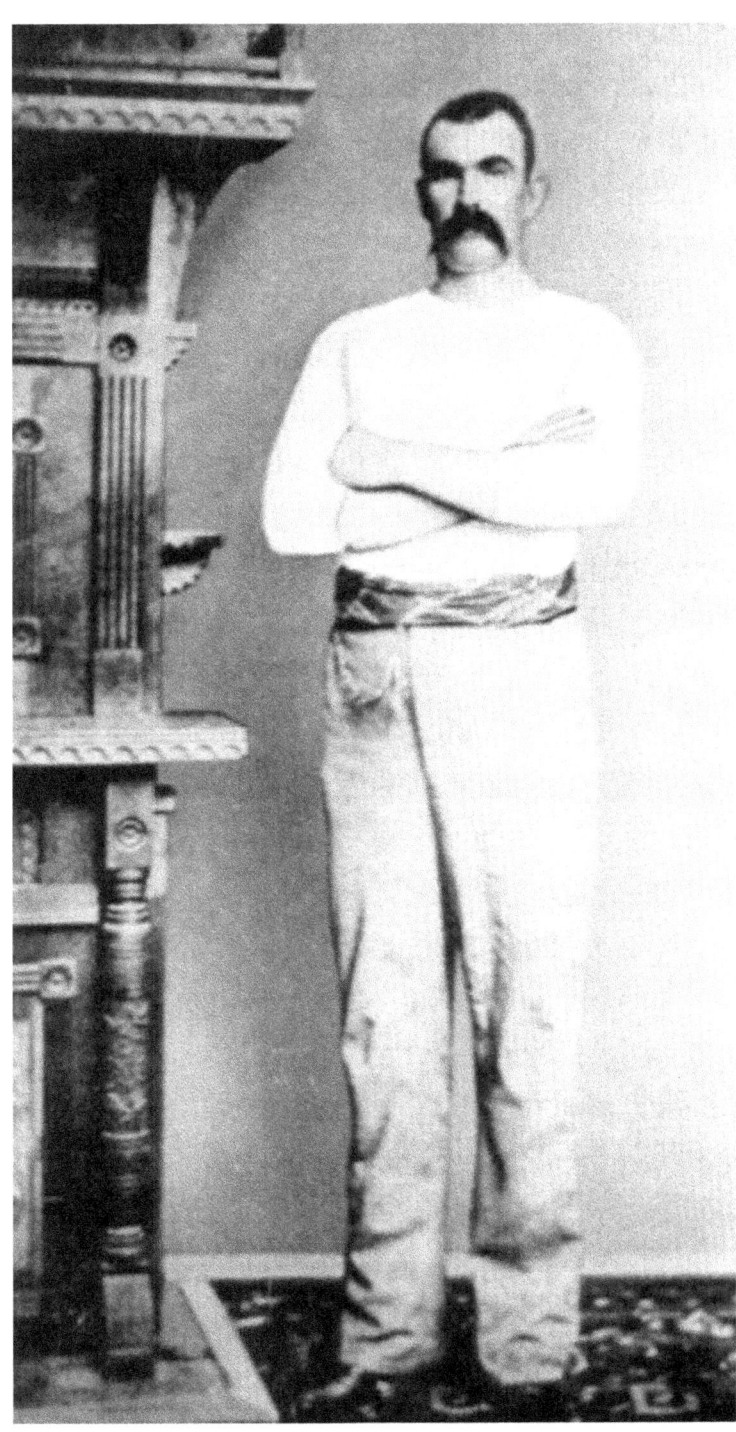

The "Old Blue Gobbler," Captain Nathaniel N. Kinney. *Courtesy of Christian County Library.*

carried them always in those days and everyone does now for that matter, while the arms of today are much better than any carried then.

Having concluded that an organization was necessary Capt. Kinney talked the matter over with several of his friends. Among them were Ben Price, Lawyer J.J. Brown (now of Ozark), J.M. Everett, and Yell Everett. "Yell" is only a nickname, his initials being B.Y., but he is known to everybody in Taney only as "Yell." His name is significant of one of the most prominent habits. Editor Patterson of the *Home and Farm*, the county paper of Forsyth, was also consulted, and he approved the idea. The consultations were held at private houses during social visits, and for a time nothing more than an agreement among friends to use their influence as citizens and property owners to have criminals punished when the evidence warranted it was contemplated. But within a month after the agreement was made, a crime was committed which convinced these men, so they now say, that there was no hope of convicting a criminal of any influence in the county by the ordinary means adopted by good citizens in ordinary law-abiding ways. The opponents of the Bald Knobbers in Taney county say that the quasi-organization was turned into a secret society to avenge the death of one of the organization's members, who, they say, was shot in a fair fight.

2

# THE MURDER OF J.M. EVERETT

Among Capt. Kinney's best friends in Forsyth was J.M. Everett. He is now spoken of among the Knobbers as a prominent merchant of the town, in the liquor business. The friends of the man who killed him say he was running a gin mill—like Capt. Kinney's in Springfield had been, and that the two men were toughs together. Everett's saloon was on the east side of the public square in Forsyth. It was a deep one-story building that had been built for a country store. There were two rooms fronting the street, the side room under the low shed roof being occupied by a billiard table. The bar was in the main part of the building.

On Sept. 22, 1883, Al Layton and Sam Hull were playing billiards in Everett's place for the drinks. At the end of each game they took whiskey straight. It is asserted that the whiskey was homemade and duty free. The Bald Knobbers deny this. No one denies that the quality of the whiskey was of the sort called forty-rod.

After three or four games, Hull "got it on to Layton in a way that he despised" as his friends say, and Layton started in to teach him that no cheating would be tolerated among gentlemen. Both men were good fighters, but Hull began to take the part of the instructor, rather than that of the pupil. Then Layton "drew his gun," which here means that he drew his revolver.

Then Saloon Keeper Everett jumped on him and threw him down. In fighting, the men had come from the billiard room, through the bar room, and out on the veranda, it was here that Layton was downed. As Everett

An 1888 newspaper illustration of Everett's Saloon. *Library of Congress.*

pinioned Layton down on the floor of the porch, he said, "I don't 'low to hurt ye. I aim to keep ye out o' trouble. I hain't got any weapon about me, Al, and ye know I wouldn't use it ef I hed."

There was a gang of interested spectators looking on at the time. Three or four advised Layton to give up his revolver, as he lay on the floor, and promised that he should not be molested further if he did so, but this he steadily refused to do. Finally one of the spectators said to Everett, "Let him up, Jim."

Everett made the mistake of doing this at once and without taking any precautions for his own safety. Layton got up, knocked the dust partly off his clothes, and then, with a wicked smile on his face, raised his pistol and shot Everett through the heart. Everett fell over against the double doors of the billiard room so violently that they were broken in. As the doors gave way, Layton fired a second shot into Everett, and then, whirling partly around, shot Yell Everett through the right shoulder, making him yell louder than he had ever done before, the witnesses say, and that was pretty loud.

Shoving his revolver into a holster, Layton leaped from the veranda into the saddle on a horse that was standing before it, and clapping spurs to the horse, he galloped out of town. A spectator said: "He didn't have no call to shoot, as I knows of. But, it was done damned slick."

At the next session of the Grand Jury, Layton was indicted in due form. Capt. Kinney was one of the Grand Jury. Layton came in and surrendered, and was admitted to bail, as is usual in this part of Missouri in such cases. At the October term of the Circuit Court he was tried.

He pleaded that he was "one in peril"; that he believed the Everetts and Hull were trying to kill him. It is charged that County Clerk Thomas Layton, who was the murderer's cousin, and Sheriff John Moseley, who was a close friend, bribed the Prosecuting Attorney to be easy with the murderer, and that they then plied the jurors with an unusually good quality of whiskey and made them drunk, and that while in this condition they brought in a verdict of not guilty on Oct. 18, 1884. There is no proof of bribery. It is admitted that the jury got drunk.

The Bald Knobbers say the acquittal of Al Layton made a tremendous sensation throughout the county. The rest say the sensation was confined to the friends of the dead saloon keeper, and that Everett's whiskey caused the whole trouble anyhow. The sensation, however big or small, was the inciting cause of the organization of the Bald Knobbers as a secret society.

# 3
# ORGANIZED AS A SECRET SOCIETY

It is commonly believed throughout the Ozarks country that the first meeting of the Bald Knobbers as a secret organization was held on the big bald peak that eventually gave its name to the Society. The fact is that thirteen men met in Forsyth, MO, first at the saloon formerly owned by J.M. Everett, but which was then run by his brother Yell. Those who are superstitious will see in the number who were present a portent of what was to come. Among the charter members were Capt. N.N. Kinney, Col. A.S. Prather, Yell Everett, J.B. Rice, T.W. Phillips, Capt. J.R. VanZandt, Capt. P.F. Fickle, Lawyer J.J. Brown, G.E. Branson, J.K. McHaffie, and J.A. DeLong. Editor Patterson says he was notified to attend, but having been told that it was to be made an oath-bound secret society, he declined to do so. This meeting was held in January, 1885. It was there formally voted, Capt. Kinney being in the chair, to make the order secret. Lawyer J.J. Brown was appointed a committee to draw up the form of an oath for members, and Capt. Kinney to prepare the constitutional by-laws.

J.A. DeLong, who was Captain of a company of forty-four Bald Knobbers afterward, says the next meeting was held on the great bald peak, the bald knob of the county, which is situated about eight miles west of Forsyth. It was held in April, but he declined to give the day, which was April 5, 1885. Capt. Kinney went there alone very early in the morning.

This peak was chosen because it commanded a view of the country for miles around, and no one could get within half a mile of the summit from any direction without being seen by any one there. The members were thus enabled to say that they meet openly where any one could see them, but the fact is that no one who had not been invited was allowed to approach, and three farmers who came uninvited were told that if they wanted to come in they must wait until the next meeting. In Mr. DeLong's paper of Sept. 27, 1888, is an article describing the first meeting. He says, as a charter member, that it is accurate.

With fear and trembling a few of the most venturesome approached the spot in horror lest they should be [led] into a trap. As they approached cautiously at the edge of the opening, they found a man who was typical of the cause in which they were expected to enlist. This was Capt. N.N. Kinney, a man who was [as] fearless as he was active, a giant in stature and as straight as an arrow. He had been a pioneer all his life, and was the owner of a large cattle ranch and had been a sufferer of the desperations of the lawless men who infected the section until forbearance ceased to be a virtue. With only a half dozen of the best citizens of the country around him, he then and there planted the seed which grew into what is to-day known as the organization of Bald Knobbers.

The reference to half a dozen men going there in fear and trembling makes the opponents of the Bald Knobbers snort with disgust. They say that the men rode up to the peak on horseback, and that each one was greeted by Capt. Kinney in person half way down the peak. All whom had been invited were present; the throng numbered nearly a hundred. Capt. Kinney made them a speech to brace them up. This speech, as near as those who heard it can recollect, was a blood-stirring oration over the bloody shirt of J.M. Everett and the crimes and immorality that had been allowed to go unpunished. It ended thus:

> *What will become of our sons and daughters! Our lives, our property, and our liberty are at stake. I appeal to you, as citizens of Taney county, to say what we shall do. Shall we organize ourselves into a vigilant committee and see that when crimes are committed the laws are enforced or shall we sit down and fold our arms and quietly submit?*

There was a motion in due form that a "vigilant committee" be organized. Chairman Kinney said, "Are you ready for the question?"

"Boys, she pops," said a facetious member of the crowd. The saying is common enough among the mountaineers, but it struck the fancy of the crowd at this time, and "Boys, she pops" was thereafter adopted as the "Aye" of the members. This was the second time they had agreed to organize.

Lawyer Brown then brought out the oath he had prepared and read it over aloud. It was approved by all. Then the men joined hands in groups of thirteen and each repeated it as follows:

> *Do you, in the presence of God and these witnesses, solemnly swear that you will never reveal any of the secrets of this order, nor communicate any part of it to any person or persons in the known world, unless you are satisfied by a strict test or in some legal way, that they are lawfully entitled to receive them: that you will conform and abide by these rules and regulations of this order, and obey all orders of your superior officers or any brother officer under whose jurisdiction you may be at the time attached nor will you propose for membership or sanction the admission of any one whom you have reason to believe is not worthy of being a member, nor will you oppose the admission of any one solely on a personal matter.*
>
> *You shall report all theft that is made known to you, and not leave any unreported on account of his being a blood relation of yours, nor will you willfully report any one through personal enmity.*
>
> *You shall recognize and answer all signs made by lawful brothers, and render them such assistance as they may be in need of, so far as you are able or the interest of your family will permit; nor will you willfully wrong or defraud a brother, or permit it if in your power to prevent it.*
>
> *Should you willfully and knowingly violate this oath in any way, you subject yourself to the jurisdiction of twelve members of this order, even if their decision should be to hang you by the neck until you are dead, dead, dead.*
>
> *So help me God.*

Although these charter members took the oath while clasping hands, those subsequently initiated had a different sort of ceremony. Charles Graves, a member of the Christian county branch of the order, testified under oath that when he was initiated he was told, before taking the oath, that once in the order there were but two ways to get out of it. Mr. Graves said:

> *One way was at the muzzle of a gun and the other at the end of a rope. There was a belt put around my neck representing a rope, and a pistol put to my breast, and I was told to hold my right hand up and put my left hand on my heart, and then the pledge was administered.*

The oath alone was the product of Lawyer Brown. The claptrap ceremony was devised by Capt. Kinney, who very well knew what would make the deepest impression on the minds of the mountaineers. Having taken the oath, the assembly then considered what name they should adopt. It is said that Mr. J.R. VanZandt who had been a member of the State Legislature, proposed the name of Bald Knobbers, taking the idea from the bald peak on which they were standing. His suggestion was adopted by vociferous acclamation.

Of course there must needs be grips, passwords, &c. The work of getting into a meeting when held by day was nothing, for the members were all personally acquainted with each other. At night the Captain of the band had to go to the place of meeting first. Then as each member approached he was required to whistle as long as possible without varying the note. This done the Captain said: "Who goes there?"

A member answered, "Bell!"

The Captain asked, "Whose bell?"

A member answered, "My bell."

One Knobber told *The Sun* newspaper reporter that the last answer was properly, "Your bell." That was the original answer, but "My bell" was subsequently used altogether.

The first rule for the governing of the order proposed by Capt. Kinney was that nothing should thereafter be written. No mark or written sign was ever made after the oath had been committed to memory and the written document destroyed. The next rule was that when anything was to be done by the original organization or any of its branches the matter had first to be referred to the chief of the county organization, who was to lay it before a council of five, and thus the course to be pursued was adopted. This rule very quickly fell into disuse, however, and a majority vote of those present decided what should be done.

When work had to be done masks were necessary to prevent the victims from recognizing their assailants. It was intended one might almost infer from the large number of dead and small number of wounded, that not many of the victims should ever live to appear as witnesses against their assailants. Still accidents might and did happen, and masks were provided for. These were of two sorts, varying only in the way they were ornamented. A black cambric skullcap was first made that fitted over the top of the head and down to the eyebrows. From this a flap descended over the face and down to the breast. Holes were cut for the eyes and mouth, and these holes were stitched around, buttonhole fashion, with red thread. Then on top of the skullcap two cones made of black cambric were sewed, the bases of the cones being stiffened with corks or plugs of wood. The point of the cone

Masked Bald Knobbers in the 1919 movie *Shepherd of the Hills. Creative Commons.*

had a tassel of red thread on it. The cone was from four to six inches long, and looked like a horn. Then a circle of white paint was drawn around the eye and mouth holes, and streaks of white paint to represent rudely a beard were drawn from the mouth hole down to the end of the flap. Some had no paint on them, however. The newly initiated members had to pay twenty-five cents each to the Captain of the band for the masks.

## 4

# THE KNOBBERS BEGIN WORK MILDLY

On Oct. 7, 1884, when the trial of Al Layton for killing J.M. Everett was just coming on, a farmer, about 40 years old, named Amus Ring, was shot dead by Newton W. Herrell, a young man of 23. Ring was living with young Herrell's mother, a widow, without having taken the trouble to marry her. The young man did not like it. Not that there was any disgrace attached in that community to the connection. Herrell was simply disgusted at his mother's lack of taste in "taking up with a no-account." Ring was not an attractive man to any one besides Mrs. Herrell, and that was a lucky thing for her son Newton.

On the day of the killing, the young man went to the house where Ring and Mrs. Herrell lived. It was a log cabin, two miles up White River from Forsyth. He had told Forsyth people that he was going to fix the old man as soon as he could get an excuse for doing so. He carried a revolver with him. He had no difficulty in picking a quarrel, for he no sooner began calling the old man obscene names than the old man picked up a stick of stove wood and told the young man to leave the place or take a good beating. Then Herrell gleefully pull[ed] out his revolver and shot the old man dead. One bullet did the job instantly.

The miserable old woman, the mother of the young man, and the only witness of the shooting, went to Forsyth and had her son arrested for murder. He was imprisoned in the Forsyth jail. Here he remained until April 7. The Knobbers had organized on the big bald knob two days before, and were anxious to let people know that they had their decks cleared for action with the black flag flying over the taffrail. Accordingly, at 10 o'clock on the night of the 7th, they rode into town nearly 100 strong, and with military precision, formed a hollow square about the jail. All were masked and armed. A squad waited on the Sheriff and brought him to the jail, where he was ordered to open the door, that young Herrell might be taken out and hanged. The Sheriff, all in a tremble of fear, begged them not to do it. At this the prisoner began to understand that there was a mob without that proposed to hang him. Throwing himself on the floor he began to scream incoherently, but in a voice that was heard half a mile away.

The Knobbers, however, had no intention of doing more than frighten him and the officials this time, and so, after gratifying their love of claptrap, by hanging a very impressive noose over the door of the jail and another over the Judge's bench in the court house hard by, they formed in line and received and obeyed the order: "Break ranks, march."

Herrell obtained a change of venue to Greene county at the next session of the court (August term). He broke out of the jail in the county seat there (Springfield), but was afterward recaptured, tried, convicted on his mother's testimony, and sent to the State prison for fourteen years. This was the first crime committed in Taney county that had ever been lawfully punished by more than two years' imprisonment.

*5*

# THE KNOBBERS' FIRST LYNCHING

A number of years ago a family of the name of Taylor came to Taney county from Kentucky, and settled in the most barren portion of it on what is known as Nubbin Ridge. Their home was about five miles from Forsyth, and was near the county road leading from Forsyth to Ozark. There were four boys in the family, two of whom very soon acquired an evil reputation among the people of the county. Their names were Frank and Tubal. The old man was of good repute, but Frank and Tubal were given to petty crimes of all sorts, such as chicken stealing, fighting and carrying concealed weapons.

Naturally people who suffered from the depredations spoke harshly of the boys, and this sort of talk was promptly resented by the boys with fresh outrages. After a while the boys found that people were afraid of them. It then became a habit with them when coming to town, to run their horses down the road to the public square, firing revolvers and yelling like Comanches or cowboys, and thus driving everybody off the streets. It afforded the Taylor boys no end of amusement since no greater damage was ever done than the breaking of a window or the splitting of a weather board or shingle by a stray bullet; no one complained.

But finally Mr. A.C. Kissee a ranch owner, got the ill will of the boys by talking about them, and they took revenge by cutting the tongues out of three fine cows which he had on his place. Having obtained proof that Tubal Taylor did it, Mr. Kissee had him indicted and arrested. This was early in the year of 1884. But as Tubal was brought into town he broke away from the officers and escaped in the dense scrub oak bushes. The search that was made for him was not of a very vigorous sort but it served to keep the young rascal in hiding, and that satisfied a majority of the people.

Frank, however, continued to take the town in the old way, growing more bold, if possible, as time passed, until he varied his wild charge around the square on entering the town by riding directly into one or another of the stores that happened to have doors open. He was arrested once or twice for this and fined small sums.

Finally Frank got married to Miranda Garrett, a Nubbin Ridge belle, who, like most other Nubbin Ridge girls, thought Frank one of the most dashing heroes that Missouri had known since the decease of the James boys' gang. The two set up housekeeping on goods bought on credit of John T. Dickinson, who ran the Nubbin Ridge store. Mr. Dickinson charged the amount to profit and loss forthwith, hoping to save himself further loss thereby.

But on April 7, 1885, that being within two months after Frank's wedding, the young man called at the store for more goods, including a pair of boots for his brother Tubal, who was still in hiding. The Bald Knobbers had been organized in the mean time, with Dickinson as a member, and the doings of the Taylor brothers had not escaped comment at the Bald Knob meeting held on April 5. Made brave by the backing of this organization, Mr. Dickinson refused to be blackmailed. Frank flew into a passion.

Mr. Dickinson's store is in a log house room 12 x 11 foot in area, and has so much stock in it that there is room for but six customers within. When Frank had got through tearing things to pieces that day there wasn't room for one except on top of the ruins. Before leaving, Frank said he would kill the merchant if complaint were made about the ruin wrought. That did not scare Dickinson, however, for the next day he went to Forsyth, where the Grand Jury was in session, and had the young man indicted.

On the same day that Frank tore up the stock in Dickinson's store [April 7] his brother Tubal surrendered to the officers in Forsyth. He was not immediately imprisoned, but was held in custody by a deputy sheriff. While standing in front of Everett's saloon, in the afternoon, Frank rode into town fresh from the wrecking of Dickinson's store. Stopping before the saloon, he got off the horse, while Tubal jumped from the high veranda of the saloon into the saddle and with a yell rode away. The Bald Knobbers, it will be remembered, came into town that night (the 7th) and frightened young Herrall out of his wits. It was because of the talk about the Bald Knobbers that Tubal regretted that he had surrendered and took advantage of his brother's arrival to leave town, Frank was arrested for aiding a prisoner to escape, but was permitted to give bail, and followed his brother Tubal out of town.

News travels with mysterious rapidity in this wild region and within two hours after Frank had been indicted at Forsyth for wrecking Dickinson's store, or by 4 o'clock on the 8th, he and his brother Tubal had heard all about it. Why they waited until next day for their revenge no one knows, but they did. About 2 o'clock in the afternoon of the 8th they went to Dickinson's store accompanied by Elijah Sublett, a young clap who had "toted grub" to Tubal when he was hiding in the woods from the officers.

Frank led the way into the store. Mr. Dickinson was seated on a little bench by the store and Mrs. Dickinson was standing behind a little counter on one side of the room. Frank walked to the bench where Dickinson was seated and sat down by him.

Frank said pleasantly, "Howdy?"

Mr. Dickinson replied, "Howdy?"

At that instant Frank grabbed the merchant by the throat with his left hand, and with his right drew a .32-caliber revolver. Jamming the revolver against his victim's mouth, Frank pulled the trigger. The ball knocked out four teeth and passed out through the neck. Then he pushed Dickinson to the floor and fired another ball into his right shoulder. Dickinson fainted, and was supposed to be dead.

Meantime Frank's brother, Tubal, and their friend, Sublett had been firing at Mrs. Dickinson. One ball took off the end off of a finger and another grazed her neck, drawing blood. She also fell in a faint and then the boys left. They supposed they had killed both of them. Of course the boys fled into the ravines of the mountains.

As soon as the news of the attempted assassination reached Forsyth, and that was very soon, a messenger hurried out to Capt. Kinney, the Bald Knobber chief. There was a hurrying to and fro for a gathering of all the members of the organization. Squads of men were sent by every possible route to head off the criminals, who were supposed to be on their way to Arkansas. Other squads scoured the ravines. It was beautiful spring weather, but the trees were in full leaf, and the task of ferreting out three men in a country that is nothing but mountain and ravine, and is covered with dense brush at that is not an easy one.

However, the work was done thoroughly under Capt. Kinney's directions, and at the end of six days, or on April 11, the trail had got so hot that the two Taylor boys gave up all hopes of escaping. Sublett was not found for several weeks, and was then sent to Springfield. Meantime, however, the Taylor boys had been told that the Dickinsons were not even dangerously wounded. They therefore concluded to surrender to the Sheriff rather than risk meeting a squad of Bald Knobbers. Word was sent to town, and Deputies T.H. Toney and Liash Yeasy went out and brought them in. They were lodged in one of the two cells of the county jail.

This jail is a hewed log hut 15 feet square. Within and without the logs are covered with two-inch oak plank. There are two doors to each cell, an inner and an outer door. Both are of oak plank. The inner door is covered with boiler iron. Both doors are secured with pad locks, the staples being made of half-inch wrought-iron rods.

At exactly 10 o'clock on the night of April 15, the Bald Knobbers, seventy-five strong, galloped down the river and into the public square. Every man was armed and masked. Except when Capt. Kinney gave an order, not a word was spoken. The orders were given in an ordinary tone of voice.

The Knobbers formed a hollow square about the jail at first, and then the chief detailed a number of men to serve as sentries about the village, the sentries being sent away in pairs. One man was sent to the blacksmith shop. He returned with two sledge hammers.

Everything had been done so quietly that the prisoners, although awakened by the arrival of the troop, did not comprehend what was happening. When the big hammers arrived they learned right away. A member of the troop began to batter the padlock and staple on the outer door. That first blow took all the bravado out of the prisoners, if it did not damage the lock much. The Bald Knobbers were terribly in earnest this time, however. After a half-dozen blows by the Knobbers, who held the sledge hammers, had failed to make any valuable impression on the lock, the stalwart chief grabbed sledge himself. Kinney was a giant in strength as well as stature. At the first blow the lock split, at the second the staple cracked half off, and at the third the lock flew ten feet away, where it was found next morning. The twisted and broken pieces of the staple and a deep dent in the door are still pointed out to the wayfarer as the work of the Knobber chief.

With each blow of the sledge hammer the prisoners within screamed for help. Their cries were heard all over the village, but no one, not a member of the Knobbers dared leave his home. When the outer lock was knocked away, the inner door was opened by prying out the staple. The prisoners, now weeping and screaming hysterically, crawled under their rough plank bunk and shrank back against the wall, as if that would save them. They were hauled out by the feet, kicking and clutching at the boards of their bunk, and the side rail of the bunk was torn away by the despairing grip of Frank Taylor before he was dragged out of the cell.

Once in the open air, they found two horses waiting for them. The Knobbers picked their prisoners as bags of corn are handled, and placed them in the saddles. Their feet were tied by ropes to the cinch straps, but not as tightly, the Knobbers say, as to make the journey painful. Then the Knobbers formed in line, with their victims in the middle, and started up the road that leads to Springfield. The voices of the prisoners begging for mercy were heard by the Forsyth people growing fainter as the procession rode away, and finally the sounds died out entirely. A few had peered out their windows and seen the prisoners writhing about on the horses in torment, but no one in the village ever saw either prisoner again alive.

It is a lonely road. It winds along between the monotonous scrub oak trees, with houses at such rare intervals as to make the stranger wonder whether there is much need of a road there at all. So small is the timber that the Bald Knobbers had to ride nearly two miles before they could find a tree with limbs large enough to sustain the weight of two men. On the top of a ridge, however, stood a tree familiar to all of them on account of its size. A long limb projected over the roadway about fifteen feet above the ground. Beneath that tree the procession halted. The prisoners were asked if they had anything to say, and if they wanted to pray to God for forgiveness for their sins. Their only answer was a continuation of their pitiful appeals to the merciless Bald Knobbers. A rope was brought to the front by one of the Knobbers. A noose was tied in each end and then the bight of the rope was tied to the long oak limb above the road. Then, while the prisoners fought desperately to prevent it a noose was placed around the neck of each, though it took three men to hold each prisoner while the noose was adjusted. While the Knobbers still held their victims, the ropes that bound their legs to the cinch strap, were cast off and used to secure the arms of the prisoner. Then, the Knobbers gave a yell, and the horses on which the prisoners had been seated trotted away, leaving them swinging to and fro and striking against each other, and intertwining their legs as they struggled in the throes of death.

It was fifteen minutes, the Knobbers say, before all signs of life disappeared. To a few of the Knobbers it seemed an awful period of almost endless duration; to the majority it was a spectacle that afforded a grim satisfaction. But not a word was spoken until the boys were dead. Then a placard was placed on the breast of one of the corpses, and the Knobbers were formed in a line and ordered to break ranks.

The next morning the villagers were astir at daylight, but no earlier. They gathered in knots about the square, stared at the broken lock and staple, on the jail doors, and talked vaguely and with painful anxiety not to offend anyone. Of 100 men who gathered there two only were found brave enough to follow the trail of the horsemen, they were T.H. Toney and A.L. Parrish. On the top of the hill they found the two victims, with faces distorted and limbs hanging straight down. On the breast of Tubal Taylor was the cover of a big pasteboard shoe box, on which had been written in rude Roman characters:

---

**These are the first Victims of**

**the Wrath of Outraged Citizens—**

**More will Follow.**

**THE BALD KNOBBERS**

---

When these two men returned and reported the facts, Justice of the Peace W.H. Jones and a Coroner's jury led the way thither, and the bodies were cut down and brought to the Court House and laid out on a table. The jury considered the case, learned what a great many witnesses didn't know about the case, and then brought in as a verdict: "We, the jury, find that Frank and Tubal Taylor came to their death by hanging, at the hands of about 100 men, to this jury unknown."

The Taylor family was then notified to come and take their dead, but this they refused to do, and the bodies were buried at the county's expense in a neglected plot called Eglinton Cemetery out on Nubbin Ridge.

Except for Capt. Kinney, who was recognized by his form, no one not with him then could say who did the duty. The lynching had been done so secretly, and withal so unexpectedly, that a tremendous sensation was created. The name of Bald Knobber became a terror to the country side for miles around, and from that time to this, except among the families of

Bald Knobbers, the name is used by foolish mothers to frighten obstreperous children into obedience.

No one will say openly, even now, who took part in the lynching, but every one of the members of the order mentioned so far was there. It is rumored that the Hon. A.S. Prather, member elect of the Legislature, furnished the rope, and that Mr. Kissee, whose cattle had been mutilated by Tubal Taylor, adjusted the nooses about the necks of the victims.

The lynching roused the fears of the friends of what the Knobbers call the old county ring. There was so much feeling on the subject however, that men on both sides sent out for weapons of modern make, and no man ventured away from home unarmed. There was little or no neutrality allowed in the county. Every citizen had to take sides in some way, and, having inspired the countryside with fear by his secret society, Kinney became at once the chief of the larger faction. People flocked to the Knobber standard for self-protection. It is interesting to note that among those who were enrolled among the Knobbers at the time of the lynching and afterward were three Methodists, two Disciple, and two Baptist preachers, as follows: The Rev. Messrs. VanZandt, Power, Spears, Owens, Johnson, Winkle, and Smith.

Still, all the victims of the Knobbers were acknowledged bad citizens, the matter of the lynching would have soon passed out of mind had not Capt. Kinney got the Knobbers to resolve that the thieves who had run the county into debt and stolen the money should be brought to justice. The thieves escaped by adding another crime to the record of Taney county—that of arson.

# 6
# TANEY COURT HOUSE BURNED

After the lynching of these Taylor boys, the Bald Knobbers held a number of public meetings, at which the condition of affaires in the county was discussed. The public meetings always followed secret meetings on the knob. At one of these, held soon after the lynching, a petition was drawn up and signed praying the Circuit Court to appoint a man of known integrity living in another county to examine the Taney county books. The late Judge Geiger heard the petition and granted it. Along in November, 1885, the man appointed went down to Forsyth to get an idea of the amount of time required for the job, and then appointed a day early in January when the investigation should begin. The ring of county officers, according to the Knobbers, consisted of County Clerk Thomas A. Layton and his assistant Sampson, Sheriff John Moseley, Prosecuting Attorney T.C. Spellings, and County Judge J.J. Reynolds. These men said they were very glad to have the stranger examine the books, because it would show that the county affairs had been honestly administered, and thus the Bald Knobber slanders would be squelched.

But the investigation was never allowed to take place. On the night of Sunday, Dec. 19, 1885, the floors and stairway of the building were saturated with kerosene oil and a fire was built in a closet under the stairway. The fire was probably started at about 11 o'clock. At midnight some citizen was awakened by an unexpected light that shone in at his bedroom window, and on looking out saw flames bursting from every window on the north side of the building. Before very many people arrived the roof was in flames.

Among the first to reach the building was Thomas A. Layton, the clerk. He burst in a window on the south side of the building, and although the room was all on fire, he got out one book that happened to be lying on the table near that window. It was an abstract of the titles of the lands in Taney county and the private property of the man who rescued it. The Bald Knobbers say that strange things do happen in Taney county, and that one of the strangest of them is the circumstance that put so valuable a book in so convenient a location. Everything else in the building was destroyed. There was nothing left to investigate, Taney county must pay her debt, and she is paying it.

# 7
# NO-ACCOUNT KILLING OF BUCK MERCER

In the meantime another man had been killed. He was an opponent of the Bald Knobbers while his slayer was a deputy sheriff who had been induced to join the organization. The Mercer family lived on Nubbin Ridge, not far from the old home of the Taylor boys, who were lynched by the Knobbers. They were accused of stealing and a variety of petty offenses. Warrants were issued for two of them on a charge of disturbing public worship.

Deputy Sheriff Arter Kissee went to the cabin to arrest them. Only one of the family, Buck Mercer, was at home. Kissee tells the story of what followed. Mercer can't; he's dead.

> *Mercer saw me coming down the hallway, and got around behind the front door with a double-barreled shotgun. So I dodged around the house to get the drop on him through the back door. Mercer heard me running, and then just about that time he found that he had made a mistake in his gun. The one he had was not loaded. The other one leaned against the wall near the back door. He dropped the unloaded gun and ran for the other just as I reached the back door. But I was too quick for him, and shot him through the breast. He died at once.*

As Kissee was an officer, no investigation was held. Mercer's friends buried him in the backyard. Some of the Knobbers sent word to the other Mercer boy to come in and take his chances on a trial or hang without one. He came in and was fined $25.

When asked about the killing, Editor DeLong said, "The matter made no stir. I had forgotten to tell you about it. It was a no-account affair."

## 8

# ANDREW COGGBURN

### SHOT TO DEATH BY THE KNOBBER CHIEF

The stranger who visits Taney county and talks to the Bald Knobbers and no one else will gather the idea that the organization, if not exactly a lawful one, was wholly beneficent in its effects on the county. The Bald Knobbers say that their only acts in that county were the frightening of young Herrell, the lynching of the Taylor boys, and the procuring of a man to investigate the county books. They had intended to do more, but circumstances arose which, to their regret prevented their doing anything more. They say they never whipped any one and never ordered any one to leave the county. By this they mean that they never did these things upon a formal order by the chief Knobber and his council. They just did it informally. A gang of a suitable size for the job would get together and make matters uncomfortable for the citizen, who was obnoxious to them, and then ride away and disappear.

Among the citizens who became obnoxious to the Knobbers were the Coggburn boys, sons of John Coggburn, at the time the Master of the Masonic Lodge of the county, and a man of excellent repute. The boys were good average boys, even according to the Bald Knobbers. Lots of Knobbers had boys quite as bad, and some had worse boys. Like all other Taney county boys, they carried concealed weapons, and sometimes fired their guns in the public highway, and yelled in cowboy fashion contrary to the statute in such case made and provided. Worse than this, however, in the Bald Knobber mind, was their avowed hostility to that order. They even threatened to shoot if attacked. The Bald Knobbers determined to have the boys arrested and punished for carrying concealed weapons and threatening the lives of

# THE PIOUS BALD KNOBBERS.

Pious. An 1886 newspaper tile. *Library of Congress.*

citizens. A warrant was easily obtained, and a squad of Knobbers went with the officer to make the arrest. The boys resisted and were victorious.

A larger and more discreet squad got the drop on the Coggburns, and the two were taken before a magistrate and fined $35 each, which they paid. This was in the summer of 1885.

At about this time Capt. Kinney made up his mind to try the gentle suasion of the Christian religion, in addition to the halter and revolver, in his efforts to promote the moral and intellectual growth of his neighbors. There had never been a Sunday school in Taney county before 1885, and Capt. Kinney organized the first one. It was at the Oak Grove church, not far from Forsyth[;] Capt. Kinney, was the superintendant. Among his pupils were the Coggburn boys. The Knobbers say the boys went there solely to scoff. The rest of the community den[ies] this. The Coggburns say, however, that they did not see much religion or solemnity about a Sunday school conducted by a man who had hanged two men unlawfully, shot no one knew how many more to death, and whose chief claim to respectability lay in the clearness of his vision when looking at the sins of others.

That the Coggburns acted irreverently is not disputed, and Robert Coggburn made blasphemous responses during the service. This was during the early and conservative days of the organization, or both boys would have been severely whipped before Monday morning.

A few weeks later a Sunday school convention was held that lasted all day. The Coggburns had been warned to keep away, but they were not easily frightened. While every one there was dressed in store clothes, the Coggburns were in their shirt sleeves. The boys carried no weapons themselves, but their sisters and sweethearts carried several revolvers under their skirts for them to use in case "Old Kinney got mad at their little joke."

When Capt. Kinney reached the church and opened the door he found hanging on the inside a coat with a little coffin on it and a piece of paper with a rude sketch of a skull and cross bones pinned beneath it. Inside the coffin was a bit of paper directed "To Old Kinney," and

> **To old Kinney**
>
> **Pizen & Death —**
>
> **is his Favorite Role**

marked within "Pizen" and "Death—is his Favorite Role." A buckshot was wrapped in the paper.

The people crowded into the building, and Kinney showed the coffin and papers to everyone. The Coggburns snickered audibly. They called it a good practical joke on the Bald Knobber chief. Going to the pulpit Capt. Kinney pointed his finger at Andrew Coggburn, and said: "The man who did that is here, and he will need a box before I do."

There was no claptrap about that. It was a promise that Kinney would kill Andy Coggburn at the first opportunity that, in Taney county ethics, would warrant the deed. Everyone so understood it, and had Coggburn shot Kinney dead at any moment thereafter, provided he did not shoot from the brush, that threat would have cleared him before any Missouri court of justice. The threat proved to be a prophecy as well as a warning.

During the exercises of the morning, Capt. Kinney made the little coffin a text and scorched the boys verbally for their sins. There was a novel spectacle at the afternoon services of this Sunday school convention. Teachers and pupils came carrying loaded guns and revolvers in the right hand and the Gospel in the left. There were two mottos on the walls of the church. One read "Peace on Earth and Good Will Toward Men," the other, "God is Love." A double-barreled shotgun leaned against the wall beneath the first, and a Kentucky rifle with a broken stock that had been mended with wire was beneath the other.

There were no converts made at this meeting. Capt. Kinney, in talking of the case afterward, said, "Of course we watched each other pretty closely as time went on."

Had this occurred in the Big Sandy region in Kentucky or West Virginia, one or the other would have been shot to death from behind the brush. Business is not done in that way here. The Ozark mountaineer is not a coward by any means, although an occasional cowardly murder has been committed. Kinney and the Coggburns were of reckless courage.

They met at last after months of watchfulness, on the night of Feb. 28, 1886, at the same place—the Oak Grove church. Andrew Coggburn and Sam Snapp, a chum[, were] in attendance at the meeting. A Bald Knobber parson was in the pulpit preparing for the service. Seeing Coggburn there, a Bald Knobber ran away to tell Deputy Sheriffs K. and Branson that Coggburn was there if they wanted to arrest him on a warrant they had for him for shooting at a man named Andrew Watson Dome time before. The Bransons were told that Coggburn was armed.

At this, one of the Bransons sent his son to tell Kinney. The lad met Kinney a short distance away, and Kinney at once went home and got his revolver. There are two stories about what followed. The opponents of the Bald Knobbers say that Kinney sent in and called Coggburn out. The Knobbers say that Coggburn heard that Kinney was coming and slipped out with Sam Snapp, and lay in wait in the window of the building (it was a moonlight night) for the Knobber chief.

The undisputed facts are that Coggburn came out of the church with Snapp as Kinney was hitching his horse. Kinney walked toward the church door revolver in hand, while Coggburn walked out into the moonlight. Coggburn stepped to one side of the path and said aloud, "Who is it?"

Some one said, "Nows yer chance,"

Kinney leveled his revolver and thundered, "Hold up your hands!"

Coggburn turned, his left side partly toward the Knobber chief, threw up his left hand, and with his right drew his revolver. It was a lightning motion, but Kinney's finger was quicker. Pressing the trigger, the Knobber chief sent a bullet into Coggburn's left breast, through his heart and out under the right shoulder. The young man was leaning partly forward, but the impact of the bullet straightened him up, and over he went on his back, dead before he struck the ground. As he fell, his revolver, thrown by his swaying right arm, flew from his grasp and struck on the gravel twenty feet away behind him.

The parson in the church was just giving out the first hymn. It began with "Sweet Hour of Prayer."

The sweet hour of prayer was interrupted by the report of Kinney's pistol, and a moment later Sam Snapp walked into the church with his hands up and the muzzle of Kinney's still smoking pistol close to his head. Kinney had held him up the moment Coggburn dropped.

"That was one of the most interesting passages of my life," said the Bald Knobber in speaking of the homicide afterward. He "came clear," as they say here easily. A Bald Knobber Justice of the Peace impaneled a Bald Knobber Coroner's jury. The Bald Knobber chief told his story, not defiantly over the butt of a shotgun, as his opponents have since said, but in regretful tones as became a Sunday school superintendent under the circumstances.

Mason symbol. *Creative Commons.*

Sam Snapp was not called as a witness. He would not have heard the call had it been made. He was not in the country. He had involuntarily become an assisted emigrant. The Knobbers provided the assistance.

The Knobber jury heard Kinney's story respectfully and sympathetically. "He jest done had," said the Knobber Justice when the recital was ended, and thereupon the Knobber jury returned a verdict of justifiable homicide.

It is an interesting matter of fact that the Knobbers, many of whom were members of the Masonic order, were able to wield enough influence in the lodge to expel Worshipful Master John Coggburn from the order because he bitterly denounced the murder of his son and the acquittal of the murderer. The ties that bound the Bald Knobbers were stronger than the ties that bound the Masons in a land were Masons often do go afoot and barefoot because it is necessary to help a brother Mason.

# 9

# THE ANTI-BALDKNOBBER MILITIA

The murder of Coggburn and the acquittal of Kinney worked up the courage or rather the fears of those opposed to the Bald Knobbers to a point where they determined to organize an opposition association, which should be formed according to the laws of the State and with the sanction of the State authorities. There is no doubt in the minds of both Christian and Taney county people to whom the reporter talked that some of the men who determined to organize a militia company were thieves who had robbed the county, and were anxious to put Kinney down lest he should discover who had burned the Courthouse. On the other hand, there were men in it who believed that the condition of the county had been worse since the Bald Knobbers had organized than it was before, that more crimes had been committed and more bloodshed, and that matters were likely to grow worse rather than better. The men accused of the stealing took the lead, however.

A secret meeting had been held in the store of J.S.B. Berry, a violent anti-Knobber, who has since figured in a typical Ozark Mountain romance. The meeting resolved simply to organize a militia company. This was at about the time Buck Mercer was killed, but nothing more was done about it until after Andrew Coggburn was shot by Kinney.

At this the militia, as they have since been called, got together again. Sixty men signed an agreement to form a militia company, and William Miles Sr. was made Captain of it. Among its members were the Rev. Messrs, Haworth and Everett, Disciple ministers, and Dennison, a Methodist. A petition to Gov. Marmaduke was drawn up, in which it was alleged that "Taney county is now enjoying a reign of terror from the depredations of a band of men organized under the name of Bald Knobbers, who ride about the country at night and terrorize good citizens, many of whom have been compelled to abandon their homes and flee from the country to save their lives."

Continuing, the petition set forth in detail the acts of Bald Knobbers in Taney county, with statements colored by prejudice somewhat. The law-abiding citizens said the petition had been compiled to organize a militia company for the protection of the citizens of the county from the depredations of a mob and for the enforcement of the civil law.

Would the Governor sanction the organization and supply it with arms from the State arsenal? He would see about it.

John Sappington Marmaduke, Missouri governor, January 12, 1885, to December 28, 1887. *Library of Congress.*

In spite of the attempts at secrecy, the Bald Knobbers knew all about this organization. There was a Bald Knobber in it as a spy. As soon as Judge Reynolds left town to carry the petition to Jefferson City to the Governor, they held a public meeting in Forsyth, not as Knobbers, but as "citizens, qualified voters and taxpayers." They resolved to "earnestly protest against the organization of military company (composed as it is), believing that it will have a tendency to inflict turmoil and cause serious trouble."

There is not the least doubt that the Knobbers had reasons for this belief. One reason was that they would have felt bound to turn in and kill off the company at the first opportunity after it was organized. Another reason was, according to Lewis Robinson, a member of the militia company, that the military company was organized for the purpose of killing off the Bald Knobbers. They were going to be moderate about it, however—that is moderate according to Ozark ideas. Capt. Kinney, Deputy Sheriff Branson, William P. Hensley, Reuben Isaacs, West Brooks, A.C. Kissee, J.T. Dickinson, and Col. A.S. Prather were to be gathered to their fathers as speedily as possible. If that didn't serve to make the lesser lights of the organization burn low, then a batch of lesser lights was to be snuffed out, and then another, until the organization was destroyed. The signal for the slaughter was to be the expected lynching of William Taylor, a brother of the lynched Tubal, and Frank Taylor, who was in jail for a cold-blooded murder which will be detailed further on.

Neither this lynching nor the slaughter [was] ever added to Taney county's records. The militia never got free guns. After hearing the militia petition and the Bald Knobber protest, Gov. Marmaduke sent Adjt. Gen. J.C. Jamison, a shrewd politician, down to Taney county to investigate the condition of Ozark Mountain Society.

Jamison talked with both sides, and then called a public meeting and had a powwow. He made a speech there that tickled the local pride immensely. Then he nudged Capt. Kinney in the ribs, metaphorically speaking, and told him the Bald Knobbers ought to go through the form of disbanding.

Accordingly, on Saturday, April 10, 1886, more than 500 Bald Knobbers assembled in the public square at Forsyth, and with the music of a brass band and much speechmaking resolved "that the organization of the Citizens' Committee be dissolved."

As it was said at the beginning of this history, Capt. Kinney had a big head full of active brains. That resolution satisfied the Governor and the honest citizens who opposed the Bald Knobbers. Of course there never had been any Citizens' Committee organized. Of course the Bald Knob Society continued business at the old stand: informally.

## 10

## MURDERED FOR MONEY TO GET MARRIED WITH

Meantime, as already mentioned, William Taylor, a brother of the Taylor boys, who were lynched, was lying in the Greene county jail charged with a heinous murder, which grew remotely out of the doings of the Knobbers.

When William's brothers, Tubal and Frank, were lynched, the rest of the Taylor family got word that the climate would be more comfortable for them in another county. They moved, therefore, to Marionville, Lawrence county, a distance of sixty miles. William had never been wild; he had had a love for books, and had gone to school when he could. He had even joined the Methodist Church, but the troubles of the family plunged them into deeper poverty than before, and he was unable to continue going to school. Then, to make matters worse for him, he fell in love with Miss Lois Norman. Although she reciprocated his passion, he could not get the money necessary to set up housekeeping in suitable style, for the lady was the daughter "of one of the best citizens of Lawrence county," and it would not do to take her into a cabin not furnished with store chairs, bed, table, and dishes. To better his finances, William determined to murder and robbery.

On Feb. 27, 1886, the day before Coggburn was murdered by Capt. Kinney, it should be noticed Taylor hired a Marionville boy named Mack Dimmock, who owned a horse and buggy, to carry him over to the old Taylor home on Nubbin Ridge, in Taney county. Dimmock had no relatives in Marionville, but had a mother living in Illinois. Dimmock and Taylor drove out of town in the afternoon. Five days later Taylor drove back with the horse and buggy.

He had a bill of sale for the outfit written in his own handwriting, but signed with Dimmock's name in a different hand. He said he had given Dimmock $60 in cash and a note for $60 for the rest of the value of the buggy, and that Dimmock had gone on to Springfield, and, thence to Illinois.

Marionville people looked on this with suspicion. Taylor had not had $60 in cash to pay for the horse and buggy, and the rig was not worth above $50 in any event. Still nothing was done about it until Mrs. Dimmock wrote to a friend in Marionville to ask about her boy. Taylor was arrested. Then Deputy Sheriff S.R. Stafford went over into Taney county, and eventually found Dimmock's body in a deep gulch near Camp Spring, on the Forsyth road. Taylor had murdered Dimmock early on the night of Feb. 28, and probably at the very hour that Capt. Kinney, the Knobber chief, was shooting Andrew Coggburn to death.

Had not the killing of Coggburn brought Adjutant-General Jamison to Taney county, there is no doubt that Taylor, when brought there for trial, would have been lynched, as his brothers were. What with the feeling created by Jamison's visit and the apparent certainty that Taylor would be convicted anyhow, the young man got a lawful trial. Through a blunder of the prosecution he was acquitted. His attorney and friends at once hustled him [out] of the county, and he escaped wholly. But Miss Norman refused to have anything to do with him, and he left the country.

The connection between the Bald Knobbers and this murder is slight. It is this: Had the Taylor boys not been lynched, William Taylor would not have become so poverty stricken, and would never have met either Miss Norman or Dimmock.

## 11

# SAM SNAPP

### Murdered by a Bald Knobber

It will be remembered that when Coggburn was murdered by Capt. Kinney, a young man named Sam Snapp came out of the church with Coggburn. He was Coggburn's chum, and was run out of the county by the Bald Knobbers. When the excitement over Coggburn's death had quieted down, Snapp returned home. It was not long before he became involved in a quarrel with a Bald Knobber. He could not keep his mouth shut about the murder of his friend Coggburn. Wash Middleton was the Bald Knobber to take up the quarrel with Snapp. Some assert that Middleton was selected by the Knobbers to do up Snapp. The Knobbers deny this.

It is not disputed, however, that Middleton was on hand several times—in fact, whenever Snapp appeared at any place of public resort, the moment Coggburn was referred to, Middleton was ready to champion the Knobbers.

At last, on Sunday of May 9, 1886, a little over two months after Coggburn was killed, the two men met in front of Kintrea's store at a crossroads hamlet called Kirbyville. Two or three nights before this Sam Snapp had ridden past Middleton's house singing a doggerel refrain composed by a brother of Andrew Coggburn after Andrew was killed. It referred to Kinney and the Knobbers obscenely, and it incensed Middleton greatly. It is said that he armed himself and went to the store expressly to kill Snapp. He began to talk about the old subject at once. Some assertion made by Middleton about the Coggburn killing proved too much for Snapp's temper, and he said angrily, "You're a damned liar."

Middleton sprang to his feet, revolver in hand. Snapp was unarmed, but he jumped up, whether to run or fight no one knows. As he reached his feet

Middleton opened fire. The first ball proved fatal, but Middleton fired two more into his victim after he fell.

Middleton at once started for Arkansas, where he had a brother living, but on the way he got frightened by a report that friends of Snapp had got in ahead of him while he stopped to bid good-bye to his family. So he determined to go into Forsyth and surrender.

The Bald Knobbers had not been idle meantime, for they had sent out a Knobber deputy sheriff named William Hunt, who took Middleton over to Mincey Valley for the night and then by a devious route to Forsyth jail. Next day he was admitted to bail in the sum of $3,000 by Probate Judge Burks.

At the October term of the Circuit Court he was tried and found guilty of murder in the second degree. He was sentenced to serve forty-five years in the penitentiary. This was a stunner to him and the Knobbers, but after circulating a petition, "which was signed by all the best citizen in the county," the Knobbers got the sentence reduced to fifteen years. This was done as a matter of form partly and partly to make the hunt for Middleton less active after he should escape.

While the court was still in session, and in fact while a night trial was in progress, not more than fifty feet from the jail, a number of Knobbers, led by Middleton's son, pulled the staple that held the lock on the inner door of Middleton's cell. The outer door had been left open by Sheriff J.K. McHaffie, who was a Bald Knobber, an election having been held the fall before and a Knobbers successor to Moseley put in.

It will be remembered that an inciting cause of the organization of the Knobbers was the fact that Moseley had aided a friend—Al Layton—to escape punishment for killing a man. Middleton fled to a brother at Parthenon, Newton county, Ark. Snapp's friends offered a reward of $200 for his arrest and return to Missouri. The State authorities offered $300.

In the last week of July Detective James L. Holt, an Arkansas official, located Middleton and went to the house to arrest him. Middleton grabbed a gun, but the detective was quicker, and shot Middleton dead. Snapp's friends paid the $200, but the State still owes $300.

## 12

# REUBEN PRUITT

### Shot Dead by a Bald Knobber

The next Knobber shooting affair was a little one for Taney county. On the night of Aug. 12th, 1886, Robert Cline of Forsyth invited his friends to his house for a dance. There was a large amount of liquor on hand, and the boys got full and quarrelsome. Some were Knobbers and some were anti-Knobbers, or militia, as they are called, and they went out on the public square and fired their revolvers at each other, but they were all so drunk that no one was hurt. The reader has doubtless already observed that when the Ozark mountaineer is sober he shoots to kill, and kills.

The next day warrants for some of the shooters were issued. Deputy Sheriff George Taylor and Constable Jerry Franklin, both Knobbers, started out to arrest Sampson Barker. At Barker's house they found Reuben Pruitt who was also wanted, and who was an anti-Knobber also. The hatred between the two factions was sufficient to make Pruitt resist, and Taylor shot him through the right breast. The ball went clear through him. Pruitt got out his revolver, and fired as he fell, but missed. Pruitt got well, but had to flee to Arkansas for having tried to shoot Taylor.

## 13

# A DUEL IN THE SCRUB OAKS

Those Taney citizens who supposed that the Knobbers had disbanded learned their mistake shortly after the last shooting affray had occurred. Capt. Kinney marshaled his host to the number of over 500, and in military style scoured the country.

A tough citizen of Arkansas named James Brown, having robbed the store of Price Milum in Lead Hill, Ark., fled across the line into Taney county. On his way across the country he robbed seven different houses, but got very little besides food, which he could have for the asking at any place. A posse of Knobbers headed by James Manus turned out immediately on August 20 and chased Brown into a scrub oak patch about four miles north of Forsyth. Here, seeing that Manus had out stripped the rest of the posse and was alone, Brown turned, and the two men had a duel. Both were armed with Winchesters. The tough was the quickest and shot Manus through the body. Manus was game and fired five shots at the tough, hitting him three times. His aim was rendered uncertain by his wound, or the tough would have died then and there. As it was, he escaped with a ball through his left arm and two wounds caused by the bullets that pierced the flesh from two of his left ribs. The tough was running when he got these wounds.

When the posse came up they found Manus so badly hurt that they abandoned the hunt for Brown to care for their wounded leader. But one of their number notified Kinney, and before dark, over 500 Knobbers had been sent in squads of two to five each into the territory where Brown was known to be.

An 1888 map of counties in Arkansas where fugitives fled. *Library of Congress.*

The tough was afoot having abandoned his horse when he took to the woods, and escape was impossible. The next morning he was over taken by James Bunch and another, and shot to death like a wounded wolf in its lair.

In the afternoon of the same day, Manus died from the effects of the wound Brown had given him. His death was the sixth that had occurred during the year of 1886, and all growing, in one way or another, out of the deed of the Bald Knobbers.

# 14

# A BALD KNOBBER ROMANCE

Although he held no office in the quasi military organization of anti-Knobbers at Forsyth, the brains of the militia were in the head of J.S.B. Berry, little, lithe, swarthy, with gleaming black eyes and straight black hair. Berry was as remarkable a man in his way as was the giant chief of the Knobbers in another way. Kinney was a born leader; Berry a born adviser. Kinney was brave and impetuous; Berry revengeful and cunning. Kinney fell upon and crushed his opponents; Berry under-mined and toppled his enemies. Men dreaded Kinney as they do a tornado; they feared Berry as they do the miasma. In the end, the cunning Berry proved more than a match for the wisdom and daring of Kinney, while a trusted lieutenant who was the not altogether admirable hero of this romance escaped only because Berry lacked some of the more manly characteristics of his neighbors.

Quite as marked in personal appearance, and also quite the equal of either of the faction leaders in mental caliber, was the wife of Berry. Mrs. Berry is tall, with long wavy black hair, liquid black eyes that languished or flamed as the mood changed, a Grecian face, a form that would make a flesh and blood man sigh, and the bearing of one noble born, there was no one in southern Missouri to compare with her. That she should have married Berry was not surprising to those who knew his cunning. Neither was it surprising that after a few months of wedded life she tolerated rather than loved him with wifely devotion. She was still tolerating him, however, when the Bald Knobbers were organized, although she had been married to him seven years.

## Taney County

Berry was a merchant and hotel keeper, but not of perfect reputation, for on two occasions he was arrested for counterfeiting. He escaped punishment on each occasion by cunning and Taney county people came almost to believe at last that he and the devil were in league, and that for once the devil was good to his own.

The Knobbers say that Berry opposed them because he feared they would deliver him over to the United States authorities, and certain it was that he spent very little time at home after the Knobbers organized. In fact, they had ordered him out of the town, but he did not stay out. Mrs. Berry carried on the business when he was away. She carried on the hotel all the time.

In the camp of the Bald Knobbers, Kinney's most trusted companion and intimate friend was young Lawyer George L. Taylor. Taylor was in no way related to the Taylors who were lynched. He was a handsome young mountaineer. He was nearly six feet tall, had laughing blue eyes, a merry smile beneath a long blond moustache, and was as kindly and genial in disposition as he was handsome in form and feature. Taylor had no relatives in town, and so, after hanging out his shingle, went to board at Berry's Hotel because Mrs. Berry was the best cook in the place.

An 1888 newspaper illustration of Mr. J.S.B. Berry. *Library of Congress.*

An 1888 newspaper illustration of Mrs. J.S.B. Berry. *Library of Congress.*

What more natural than that the wife who could not be proud of her husband scarce attempted to conceal her contempt for his underhanded methods, in fact—should fall in love with the kindly and genial young lawyer? What more natural than that this kindly young lawyer should first feel sorry to see such a magnificent woman so illy mated, and then that his sympathy should develop into a hearty affection?

Mrs. Berry had no children. Small wonder, then, that marriage vows were forgotten when the husband was away, or that marriage ties became irksome when he was at home. It is the old story. The husband came home unexpectedly one night, and the lover, with little to cover him, fled through the back yards of two neighbors, while Berry tired a revolver vainly at the ghostly figure.

It is said by the veracious Knobbers that Capt. Kinney never laughed so heartily in his life as when another Knobber who had seen the escape described to him in drawling tones the picture of Taylor leaping in wild haste over rail and picket fences, while Berry leaned far out of one of the hotel windows, cursing like a pirate and working the trigger of a double-action revolver.

Circumstances alter cases. The over-affectionate natures of some of his neighbors had been one of Capt. Kinney's chief arguments for the organization of the Bald Knobbers. Here was a Bald Knobber who was unlawfully affectionate. Would Capt. Kinney have him expelled and run out of the county? Secretly, Capt. Kinney was the young man's ardent friend in the trouble that followed, and did more than anyone else could have done to protect the young man from the penalties of the law, for Berry appealed to the law as well as the revolver for redress.

It is not a little singular, considering the country, or rather the people, that after seeing his wife in Taylor's arms and chasing the young man from the house with a revolver, Berry should have next day met the young man and discussed the case with him. Not that intimacy of this sort is such a heinous offence in Taney county, but because the rule here is that when once a man has "drawed a gun" on another, both must go armed thereafter and shoot at sight.

But Taylor did not want to kill Berry, even if he were of the militia, while Berry was trying by cunning and deceit to act Taylor out of the war. The discussion ended in Berry's accepting a challenge to go down on the river bank the next morning [Tuesday, July 2, 1888] and fight a duel, man fashion, with revolvers. Berry never dreamed of carrying out the agreement, however.

As night came on, he loaded a shotgun with buckshot and sat out on the porch in front of his store that faces the square on the east side. About sixty yards away to the southwest is a public well. As dusk came on, Berry saw Taylor approached the well, jumping from the hitching post twenty yards nearer to Taylor. Taylor saw him, and, drawing a revolver, sprang behind the well curb and fired five rapidly. The Bald Knobbers talk about this reluctantly because Berry was not hit. Then Berry fired one barrel of his gun at Taylor. The other cartridge did not explode, and so Berry drew and fired once. At this Taylor ran ignominiously and the battle was over.

Berry then left town, and Taylor became Mrs. Berry's lover until Berry returned. This time Berry resorted to the law. Warrants charging Taylor and Mrs. Berry with adultery were obtained, and the case came in before the justice Lindsey at Kirbyville. Taylor drove over to the trial in the centre of a big wagon load of Knobbers, every one [of] whom was aroused with revolvers and several repeating rifles. Berry went with a load of rifles equally armed. In the court room it was the Justices duty for security by itself, with the one they were guarding behind the rest. All sat with fingers on their pistol triggers.

Mrs. Berry, surrounded by a group of Knobber ladies, smiled brightly toward the Knobber group. She sat with her back toward the other group. She denied the accusation indignantly. Nearly everybody in the court pretended to believe her. Even the militia despised Berry for resorting to the law, and he would not have had a friend or a guard but for the fact that Taylor and his friends were Bald Knobbers.

The Justice adjourned the case by agreement of counsel, and the parties went home. Berry drove home ahead of the other party and started out across the square with his attorney, Lawyer "Babe" Herrington, now of Ozark village, the rest of his guards having gone away. Then Taylor arrived and discharged his guards at the corner of the square and walked down to Hilsabeck's hotel. There he saw Berry near the corner of the jail, and fired one shot at him. The bullet hit Lawyer Herrington's trousers. Berry fired back three times and hit the hotel, in front of which Taylor stood, just once. It was very disgusting to the mountaineers to see such wretched marksmanship.

On another occasion Berry fired from the inside of the store, through his own window, with a rifle, at Taylor, who sat on the Hilsabeck house portico. The ball pierced the brim of Taylor's broad-brim hat, and the weatherboarding behind it. A disgusted Knobber called the reporter's attention to both holes of last week, for Taylor still wears the hat.

The outcome of it all was that Mrs. Berry got a divorce from Berry and moved to Galena, Kansas, where she now is. The business went into a receiver's hands, and Capt. Kinney was appointed receiver. Berry remained around long enough to take part in the killing of Capt. Kinney, but not long enough to take off Taylor, as he hoped to do, because, meantime, A.S. Prather, Taylor's lawyer, had entered a plea of guilty in the adultery case, and Taylor, had left town to avoid the penalty.

He came back, after Kinney was killed, but has never been called on to suffer any penalty for the crime of which he acknowledged himself guilty. But he is less popular, it should be said, with the Knobbers since he confessed the guilt that the woman continued to deny.

It is interesting to note that among Berry's guards were Detective Holt and William Miles Jr. whose father had been Captain of the militia. A brother of William Miles swore at the trial that he had twice seen young Taylor in Mrs. Berry's bed.

This testimony, on account of circumstances not necessary to relate, was obviously false, and Capt. Kinney said in open court that the young man had perjured himself. Berry took advantage of this assertion and the anger it excited to get William Miles to commit a crime he was too cowardly to commit himself, the murder of the hated Knobber chief.

*15*

# KNOBBER CHIEFTON DIES—
# WITH HIS BOOTS ON

The last of the hearings in the trial of young Taylor and Mrs. Berry for adultery was held during the week ending on Saturday, the 18th of August, 1888. It was in the course of this week that Capt. Kinney called young Miles a perjurer. In the mean time, on the application of Mrs. Berry, Kinney had been appointed a receiver for the Berry business in a suit for a partition of the property, of which Mrs. Berry owned a share in her own right. After the trial, Mr. Berry brought the Miles boys to Forsyth (their home was on Nubbin Ridge) and kept them about him as a body guard, he said, to protect him from Taylor's friends. He was really plotting to kill Capt. Kinney, whom he hated on general principles, because the Knobbers had ordered him out of town, because Kinney helped Taylor on the trials, and because Kinney was now in charge of the business.

Acting on Berry's advice, the Miles boys concealed their anger over Kinney's charge of perjury. On Saturday, the 18th, they were in and out of the store where Kinney was in charge and talked socially.

On Monday morning Aug. 20th, Kinney came to town and opened the store at about 8 o'clock. He was at work about it for an hour or so in his shirt sleeves, for it was a warm morning. At about 9:40 o'clock he walked into the office of the *Taney County News*, run by his stepson, Prosecuting Attorney J.A. DeLong. At about this time Berry came into the *News* office, carrying a Winchester, as usual. The three men talked for a moment or two and then Kinney went out. Mrs. DeLong was there also. Berry took a seat about four feet away from DeLong, who was writing the story of the previous week's trial of young Taylor and Mrs. Berry.

It never occurred to any one that Barry was in there watching DeLong to see that he did not go into the store for a time, but that was the fact and had DeLong followed Kinney into the store at any time within twenty minutes, Berry would have shot at him. It is too much to say that DeLong would have been hit.

At precisely ten o'clock five heavy pistol shots were heard in the store in rapid succession. DeLong and Berry jumped up. Berry being a deal more anxious over the matter than DeLong, for the latter never dreamed of anyone getting the drop on the Knobber chief. Out the door they went, and on the portico of the store, together with half a dozen others who had been idling about.

William Miles Jr. met them at the door with a smoking pistol in hand. Leveling this in the faces of the men, he swore he would shoot any one who failed to leave the porch. All of them stepped off save Berry, who slipped into the store. Miles then threw open his pistol, ejecting five empty shells and one cartridge, and deliberately loaded the cylinder again, while the spectators looked at him without offering to interfere. DeLong says no Knobber tried to shoot Miles, because the county officers were all Knobbers at this time, and the prospect of a fair trial, i.e. conviction, was good.

When the pistol was loaded, Miles said, "Jest step in, gents. You'll see I done it in self-defense."

The "gents" stepped in. It was plain that Kinney had stooped to pick up a butt of tobacco from the floor, but hearing Miles enter the store had risen almost to an erect posture, when Miles had leveled a big revolver and fired. The bullet struck him, in the left breast, in the exact location where

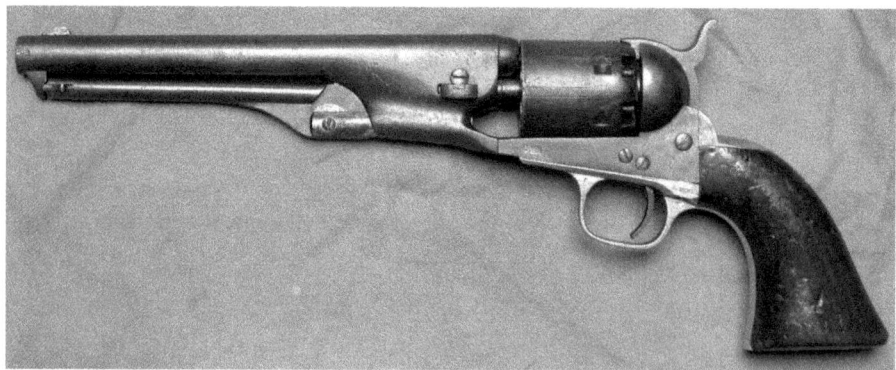

An 1861 navy Colt revolver, .36 caliber. *Creative Commons, Hmaag.*

Kinney's bullet had struck young Coggburn two years before, and straightening the Chief up, had hurled him over on his back, dead before he reached the floor. But Miles had not enough confidence to stop at that. He fired four more shots, one of which hit the dead Chief's right forearm, and two pierced his abdomen. The other missed the mark entirely.

Kinney had often said he hoped to die with his boots on. His wish was gratified.

In a pool of blood by his side lay a heavy navy revolver. No cartridge had been fired. Young Miles called the attention of the "gents" to it, and said Kinney had drawn it on him first.

An 1888 newspaper illustration of Captain Nathaniel N. Kinney, born 1839, New York. Died August 20, 1888, Taney County, Missouri. *Library of Congress.*

There are two sufficient reasons for [not] believing this lie. Had Kinney drawn the revolver first, [Miles would have] suffered as Coggburn did. [The other was it] was Berry's revolver and not Kinney's. Kinney's was round behind the prescription cases.

Intense excitement and more bloodshed were feared, as Kinney had almost an unanimous following in the hills. After this, numerous outrages were charged to him and his death hailed much joy by the anti-Knobbers as with frenzied sorrow by the members of the old band. Among the rough people there he was king and the death of their chieftain will not go unavenged. Kinney had large following in the county and more bloodshed is looked for. The men have been at danger's points for two years past, the feud dating from the time when Kinney was chief of the outlaw kind and ruled with a rod of iron. The two men at a Republican rally in Ozark quarreled and were separated. Later the quarrel was renewed.

Miles escaped unhurt. A message was sent to Harrison, Arkansas, for blood hounds to track the murderer, and there excitement over the affair never before equaled in the Bald Knob hills.

Miles and Berry were arrested. A guard of four Knobbers and four militia kept watch over them for two days. They waived examination then and were admitted to bail in the sum of $5,000. Then the Grand Jury indicted them, and Judge Hubbard arraigned them. During the sitting of the Grand Jury, thirty Knobbers kept guard lest the militia should rescue Miles soon as the indictment was found. No attempt at rescue was made, however, Judge Hubbard fixed the bail at $5,000. The bail was furnished. Prosecuting Attorney DeLong said, "The bonds are good, and they are the only really good bonds ever given in this county."

It is interesting to note that after Berry was arrested, Mrs. Berry, who had meantime got her divorce, mortgaged a farm she owned in the White River valley for all it was worth and the money for Berry to defend himself with, and Berry accepted it. That's the kind of a woman Mrs. Berry is.

William Marion "Bill" Miles is only 23 years old. He was born in Scott county, Virginia, 1867. His family removed to Taney county, Missouri, in 1871, and settled near Taney City what is now called "Nubbin Ridge," from the soil being very sterile. Here Miles grew to manhood, his time being principally devoted to hunting and fishing, at which he became very expert. He was 10 years old when he first went out to hunt with his father's rifle. The schooling in Taney county was very poor and the game was good. The forests were full of deer, turkey, squirrels, in short, all kinds of game, while the youngster found excellent fishing in the White river.

At 12 years of age he bought a revolver, which he carried sub rosa for two years. When he was 16, he discontinued carrying it, but resumed it when the Bald Knobbers organized in Taney county. He seems to have a natural predilection for firearms, and during that period in which he carried a revolver, he practiced shooting daily at any mark he could find. It is not remarkable that he at last became expert, enough to drop the Bald Knobber chief.

Miles went to Texas for a year during the Bald Knobber troubles in his county, but returned. He is quite a hero among the Christian county victims of the Bald Knobbers. All who have been whipped by Bald Knobbers admire him, and he has no trouble whatever in raising bail. Miles appreciates his sudden distinction, and when sitting for a photograph, had it taken with his revolver across his breast. At this his attorneys demurred, whereupon he promised to have no more pictures taken in such an attitude.

Kinney has left a wife and two children, the youngest [of] whom is a beautiful girl of 16. The widow is rapidly grieving her life away, for she was faithful and affectionate in a country where faithfulness is at best rare. His stepson Editor DeLong, loved him as a father, and cannot now talk of him for any length of time without being noticeably affected.

## 16

# SPLIT IN THE ORDER OF PISTOLS

1889.—About a year ago the whole Bald Knobber region in southwestern Missouri, the center of which is Taney county, was stirred up over the shooting to death of Capt. N.N. Kinney, the man who organized the order. Capt. Kinney was shot on Aug. 21, 1888, by William M. Miles, a young man of 23. People who were acquainted with the history of the Bald Knobbers predicted at that time that the death of Capt. Kinney would stop all the trouble, but it has been smoldering ever since, and recently broke out afresh when the three Miles boys, Manuel, William M. and Jim, shot and killed Sheriff Branson and Detective Funk at Kirbyville, near Capt. Kinney's old home, on July 4.

Sheriff G.E. Branson was one of the original Bald Knobbers, and was associated with Capt. Kinney when the order was first formed. Capt. Kinney was originally a saloon keeper in Springfield, Mo. In 1883 he moved to Taney county, and he became very much incensed at the depredations which were committed on life, and property. It was claimed that since the close of the war all the way from twenty-two to thirty-two murders had been committed, and in no case had the murderers been punished. The lives and property of the people were in constant danger, and Capt. Kinney argued that this thing ought to be stopped. The officials of the community, on the other hand, declared that Kinney was not a person to pass judgment on the morals of a community. Capt. Kinney was warned by his friends that his life would be in danger, but he replied that he would have a finger in the pie when the time came.

In the mean time, J.M. Everett, who was one of Capt. Kinney's best friends in Forsyth, the county seat of Taney county, and who was referred to as "a prominent merchant of the town in the liquor business," was deliberately shot down by one Al Layton, who had been playing billiards in his place. Layton fell into a dispute with one Hall with whom he was playing, and while they were fighting Everett came out and separated them, holding Layton down. Finally, however, he let Layton up, a mistake on his part, for, although he was unarmed, Layton shot him dead at once. In October, 1884, a jury returned a verdict of "not guilty."

## The Present Difficulties

The origin of the present difficulty began some time ago when Edward Funk and James H. Dennis, two detectives about 23 years of age, came into Taney county from Eureka Springs, Ark., and concocted a scheme to entrap Arbert Combs and Austin Stockstill, two young men who were members of two powerful and numerous families in Taney county, by inducing them to rob the store of one Cummings. They did it in this wise. Funk stayed in Forsyth and Dennis went to the Stockstill and Combs settlement at the mouth of Bear creek and hired out as a farm hand. He ingratiated himself into the graces of young Combs and Stockstill, represented himself to be a tough character and finally proposed that the trio rob the Cummings store. The two victims fell into his trap. Then he told Cummings about it, got his keys to the store and arranged to have Sheriff Branson and Funk near by on the night of the attempt.

The night came around, and Dennis unlocked the door with the keys Cummings had given him and sent Combs and Stockstill inside to gather the plunder while he stayed outside as he said to keep watch. When the robbers had entered the store Dennis gave the signal, and they were rushed on by the two detectives and the sheriff. Combs ran out and on his way shot Dennis dead. The next day he was arrested for murder; Stockstill was caught in the store. At the inquest held over the body of Dennis, Funk made a violent speech and justified the course pursued by his dead friend in entrapping Combs and Stockstill.

The entire Combs and Stockstill families who had been zealous Bald Knobbers and supported Branson for sheriff, now turned around and denounced him for favoring the methods of Dennis and Funk, and thus there resulted a split in the Bald Knobber element. The feeling against Funk became very strong, for the people did not endorse their patent burglar trap.

Thus we have two parties. On one side Sheriff Branson, one of the original Bald Knobbers, Detective Funk and their sympathizers; on the other side the Miles boys, the Combs and Stockstill families and their sympathizers. It was natural therefore that on the Fourth of July the day of the celebration at Kerbyville when both parties were brought together some trouble should ensue.

## A Lively Fourth

On the Fourth of July the Miles boys went to Kerbyville immediately in the neighborhood of Capt. Kinney's old home. Sheriff Branson accompanied by Detective Funk went to the celebration at Kerbyville also. Nothing happened as an indication of the coming tragedy until about 4 o'clock in the afternoon, when some one came and told the sheriff and Funk that the Miles boys were displaying pistols at the spring. The sheriff and detective started to the spring see what the Mileses were doing. Funk was some distance ahead of Branson, and accosted Bill Miles first, asking him his name and demanding his arms. It is claimed by the friends of Branson that no violence threatened, and that the intention of the officer was merely to disarm the Mileses in discharge of his duty.

Before Funk had more than made known his business it was asserted by the Branson faction that Jim Miles drew his pistol, and, stepping to the rear of the detective, shot him in the back. As Funk reeled and turned, Jim fired again, the ball entering the right side, both shots being fatal. By this time Branson had advanced within five or six steps of the Mileses, and Bill opened fire on the sheriff, his first shot striking the cheek under the left eye, penetrating the brain and lodging against the skull, a little forward of the right ear. The next shot from Bill Miles' pistol struck Branson in the leg below the knee.

The friends of Branson consider the killing deliberate murder. The militia party hold that there was a plot formed to kill the Miles boys and that the latter acted in self-defense.

Jim, who was wounded, was carried some distance by his brothers but was finally captured and taken to jail. After Bill had traveled around several days, he was finally taken in the vicinity of Springfield.

## Hundreds on the Hunt

Three hundred armed men were out day and night hunting William Miles, who killed Sheriff Branson, of Taney county, on the Fourth of July. James Miles was placed in jail, and it was not thought that he would live, as he had a very bad shot above the right hip, ranging downward, and inflammation had commenced. Forsyth was on the war path, and every man you see has either a gun or pistol. Guards are out on all the roads for fifteen or twenty miles, but having no trace of the assassin so far; but the supposition was that [William] was with his brother the night before [James] was arrested, thought [James] would not get well and went on and left his brother to die.

It is the opinion that this last killing in Taney county grew out of the murder of Captain Nat Kinney, whom William Miles shot. It is reported that he said he had six more men to kill in Taney county and then he would be through.

The people all seem to think that the trouble has just commenced and the old grudges that existed between the Bald Knobbers and anti-Bald Knobbers will be taken up again and Taney county will again take up arms against one another and have a war between themselves. The coroner's inquest was held the evening of the killing, and the jury gave in a verdict as follows: "We, the jury, find from the evidence that G.B. Branson and Edward Funk came to their death[s] at the hands of William and James Miles."

Sheriff Branson was a man that stood well with most of the people in Taney county and was a Bald Knobber, and his friends say they will have revenge. Last evening as the shadows of night came over the little town of Forsyth, everybody seemed to get excited as the rumor came in that they had William Miles surrounded in a bluff down the White river and quite a number of guns were fired. Miles had plenty of his friends with him and would be hard to take alive.

James Miles was called on in the jail, and in his rough little cell, he made the following statement:

> I and my brother William went to Kirbyville on the day of the Fourth, and each of us had a pistol, we thought we had a right to carry them, as our lives had been threatened. In the afternoon Funk came up to me and threw a pistol in my face and ordered me to throw up my hands. He was standing with his side to me and I thought he was going to shoot, and I fired at him and he fell. After he fell, he fired at me and made this wound that is now hurting me so bad. At this time Sheriff Branson came running up and commenced to shoot, and my brother shot him through the head, and then we were afraid of a mob and ran to the woods. I thought I was justifiable in doing what I did.

James Miles was free to talk, and did not seem to care who heard him, as a large crowd was around the jail at the time he was talking. The sheriff thought that William Miles was in the hills of White river. Bill had traveled around several days; he was finally taken in the vicinity of Springfield.

## 17

# DIFFICULTY IN GETTING A SHERIFF

July 20, 1889.—Rufus Barker and Westley Combs were arrested and lodged in the Taney County jail last Tuesday for being accessories to the killing of Sheriff Branson and Ed Funk. It is reported new that Rufus Barker did some of the shooting at Kirbyville July 4; that there was a conspiracy to kill Branson and Funk; and that more than the Miles brothers will be implicated in the murder.

Rufus Barker refused to go in jail and said he would kill the man who put him in. He could not be persuaded by the sheriff to go in the cell and the sheriff and his posse had to drag him behind the bars, Barker swearing he would have revenge.

James Miles, who was shot by Funk, says that all he wants is a fair trial—that is, if he should get well. His wounds are improving very fast and in a week or two he will be out of danger. The cell in which he is confined is very small and close, and a crowd standing around the doors and windows shuts off most of the air from the young assassin, but he says he can stand any thing now. He never flinches when his wounds are being dressed and seems to have an iron constitution.

The county court met last Saturday to appoint a sheriff and after making several appointments could not get any one to act as every man appointed seemed to be afraid and declared he would not have the office for thousands of dollars. But each side fought hard for their man—that is the two factions, Bald Knobber and militia, did. Finally a Bald Knobber, Reuben Isaacs, agreed to accept and the old coroner, Madison Day, gave him the keys and Isaacs was sworn in, saying at the same time, "I guess this will shorten my life."

The preliminary trial of Barker and Combs will come up next Tuesday, and the belief is general that Barker will be convicted, as he was seen running from where the shooting was done. The trial will likely bring out the cause of all the trouble in Taney county from the hanging of the Taylor brothers down to the killing of Branson and Funk.

About all the citizens of Taney County agree upon the danger of an outbreak there at any minute between the two factions, but many of the citizens are doing all they can to keep down disturbances. Dr. K.L. Burdette, one of the oldest practicing physicians in Southwest Missouri, and for many years a citizen of Forsythe, has felt it necessary to leave the county to save his life. He was attending Jim Miles at the jail, but suddenly left with his family.

## 18

# TRIALS & ACQUITTALS

J.S.B. Berry was acquitted on July 25, 1889, for the murder of Capt. Kinney, and held over for another trial for an assault on Taylor.

On August 14, 1889, most of the time of the criminal court in Springfield, Mo., was devoted to the cases of J.S.B. Berry and William "Bill" Miles, the former indicted as accessory and the latter as principal in the murder of the Bald Knobber chief, Captain Nat N. Kinney, at Forsyth last August. On motion of the defense, Berry's case was continued until next Monday, and on motion of the State the case of William Miles was continued until the next term of the criminal court, to be held the third Monday of next month. Berry's attorneys say they will be ready for trial next Monday. Miles' case was continued because the State asked for him to secure important witnesses who are absent in other counties. It is hinted around by the murdered man's friends that Miles' case will be nullified and [he] be arrested and tried for shooting to death Sheriff G.E. Branson at the last Fourth of July. Miles was released on a single, and placed in prison on a double.

The second trial of William Miles, at Springfield, Mo., for the murder of Capt. N.N. Kinney ex-chief of the Bald Knobbers terminated in the criminal court on March 22, 1890, at a late hour night by the jury returning a verdict of not guilty. Miles was taken to the jail again being under indictment for the murder of Sheriff Branson and Officer Funk. The defense set up a theory of self defense which together with the established reputation of Capt. Kinney for being a violent, dangerous and vindictive man secured the acquittal. Miles was taken back to jail to be tried at the next term of the Christian

County court on the charge of killing Sheriff Branson and Detective Funk at Kirbyville.

Billy and Jim Miles were acquitted for the murder this 5$^{th}$ of September by a Christian county jury. The charges were dismissed by Taney's prosecutor of the murder of Detective Funk.

*19*

# A BOY WHO DIED RATHER THAN SUFFER DISHONOR

With one exception, those who have been killed in the Knobber warfare have been hanged or shot to death. That exception was George Warren, a boy in his teens, who was stabbed to death by Claude Layton, a brother of ex-County Clerk, Thos. Layton, and cousin of J.M. Everett who was murdered by Al Layton. The story of the crime illustrates the condition of society in Taney county, for the Laytons and the Warrens unquestionably belong to "the best families in the county." Warren's father was a Knobber. That was sufficient excuse for a Layton to kill him whenever reasonable opportunity offered.

Layton had an attractive sister, who was loved by Dan Hinkle. The lass also loved Dan. Dan persuaded her that the interrelation of a person was not necessary to the consummation of love. A child was born, and Claude and Dan became friends. Such things do not call for blood in Taney county; however the union, the families are divided on the Knobber question.

Now it happened that young George Warren, who was just beginning to run with the girls, loved one of Dan's sisters.

One night in March, 1888, young Warren took his sweetheart to a church service at the Cherry Grove school house, five miles southwest of Forsyth. Claude Layton was standing outside. As Warren walked up to the door, as proud as a noble lord with his sweetheart, Layton, "jest t' be smart," said aloud that any one who would go with a Hinkle girl loved society and lewd women. The boy retorted by making a reference to Layton's unfortunate sister, and went on into church.

Pretty soon Layton sent a friend into the church to invite the boy to come out and get his get his mouth slapped for being "top society." The boy was no match physically for Layton, and was unarmed, but the Ozark Mountain boy will generally face death cheerfully, as Warren did, rather than bear the taunt of cowardice in the presence of his sweetheart. He went out immediately, saying to his sweetheart: "Good-by; Layton will kill me."

As he stepped outside, the cowardly brute who had sent for him jumped upon him with a long-bladed pocket knife and ripped his abdomen open. Layton fled. Warren died in agony [the] next day. Layton has since surrendered, and been admitted to jail. The death of Capt. Kinney and the fate of the Knobbers in Christian county has weakened the backbone of the Knobbers in Taney county, or both Layton and Miles, the slayer of Kinney, would have stretched rope with their necks before this.

# 20

# KNOBBER WIFE INSANE

## An Awful Tragedy

A brief recital of the fate of the wife and two of the children of a Knobber living on Bull Creek, about eight miles from Forsyth, will complete the record of bloodshed growing out of the Knobber troubles up to this date.

William A. Pruitt is a farmer of fair repute. He was one of the first to join the Knobbers, and because of his learning and force of character was made a leader in the organization. He therefore became an object of hatred among the militia, and has had to live, as have the rest, continually on his guard, and with arms hard by. He has never been molested, nor is he likely to be, nor does the ever present probability of a conflict with arms trouble him. Not so his wife. No one can tell, no one who has not had the awful experience, can even remotely appreciate the sorrows that have fallen on the wives of these people since the Knobbers were organized. The haggard faces, the beat forms, the tears that now flow whenever the trouble is mentioned, do but faintly indicate their sufferings. America, the wife of Mr. Pruitt, at last broke down entirely.

On Thursday, Nov. 22, 1888, Mr. Pruitt and his two sons went to a [neighbor's] to assist at some sort of work to which other neighbors had been invited. He left his wife and two daughters, both under 14 years old, at home. The wife was apparently in her usual health; she was rather more cheerful, in fact, than usual. Some hours later Mr. Pruitt sent his younger son, a boy of 16, to tell the mother that they would be home soon. After a while Mr. Pruitt and the others started home.

Halfway there they met the lad who had gone before running at the top of his speed, and gasping rather than speaking the word "father" at every step. And yet he failed to recognize either father or brother when he met them, and when stopped by his father he fell in a faint.

Leaving the boy to the care of his brother, the father ran home. In the front yard lay one daughter with her skull crushed in four places. Near the front door lay the other girl with her skull broken in like manner, and by her side lay a blacksmith's hammer covered with blood and brains. An awful trail of blood led from the rear door around the house. Along this Mr. Pruitt staggered for thirty steps, and reached the dead body of his wife, with an open, blood-cover[ed] razor in her hand, and her throat cut.

Her troubles had driven her insane, and she had killed her children with the hammer and then cut her own throat with the razor while standing before a mirror. Her blood had spurted over the mirror, but life had remained long enough to enable her to run from the house toward the creek, as if to finish her awful work by drowning.

*Part II*

# CHRISTIAN COUNTY

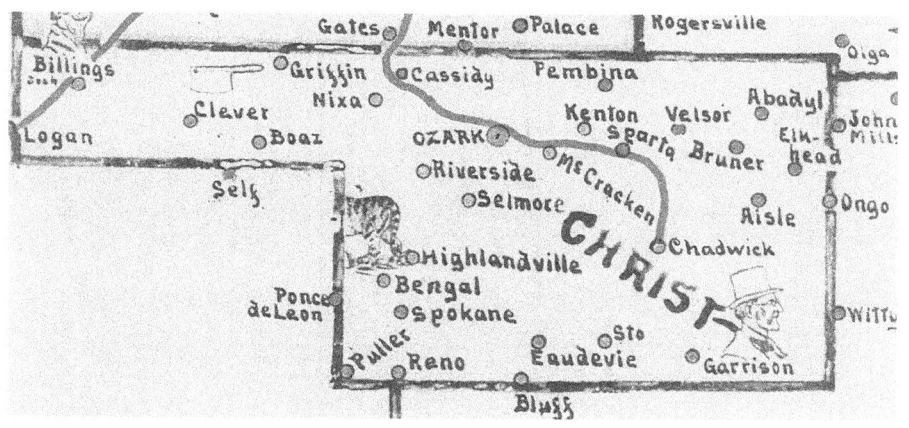

Galbraith's Railway Mail Service Maps, Christian County, Missouri, 1898. *Library of Congress.*

## 1
## CONVICTED BY HIS ASS

The sensation created when the Bald Knobbers dropped down on the jail in Forsyth and carried away and hanged the Taylor boys swept wave-fashion through the valleys and ravines of the mountains, flooding every village, splashing up beside the fireplace in every farm house, and roll[ing] across the borders of the county into the counties adjoining. Wherever its influence was felt, it set the people who were at all deeply sensible of their neighbors['] sins a pitching and plunging about like a Dutch galleon in a chopping sea.

Douglas county Pharisees received the new gospel with rejoicing, the elect of Christian county with thanksgiving, and the sanctified of Ozark county with an incense of gunpowder, after the manner in which Ozark county people always receive whatever interests or excites them.

Legions were first organized in Douglas county, then in Christian, and after that in Ozark, Stone, Howell and Greene. Of the doings of the Knobbers in all these counties no details can be given, save only in Christian county.

Let the reader picture a wretched human being dragged from his bed at midnight, pulled out over the splintered remnants of his cabin door, and then tied across the rear end of his wagon, if one were near, with a hand to each wheel. Picture wife and children on their knees in agony. Picture the Knobbers, in devilish masks and with coats and trousers wrong side out, stepping up in turn and striking the man from three to five blows each with a hickory gad, every blow of which brings the blood. Then vary the

*Above*: Galbraith's Railway Mail Service Maps, Douglas County, Missouri, 1898. *Library of Congress.*

*Below*: Galbraith's Railway Mail Service Maps, Ozark County, Missouri, 1898. *Library of Congress.*

*Opposite, top left*: Galbraith's Railway Mail Service Maps, Stone County, Missouri, 1898. *Library of Congress.*

*Opposite, top right*: Galbraith's Railway Mail Service Maps, Howell County, Missouri, 1898. *Library of Congress.*

*Opposite, bottom*: Galbraith's Railway Mail Service Maps, Greene County, Missouri, 1898. *Library of Congress.*

## CHRISTIAN COUNTY

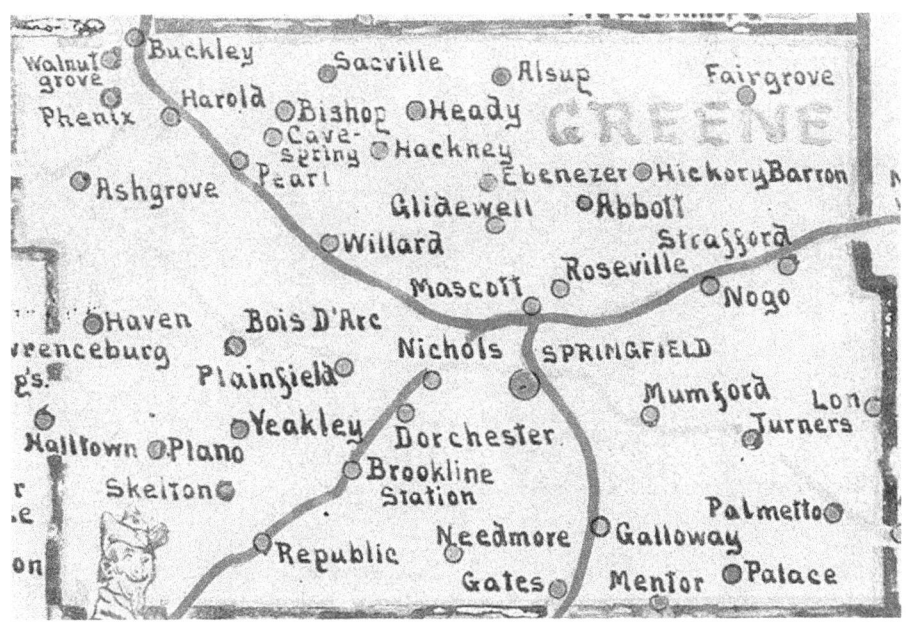

picture by substituting a woman for a man, and multiply these pictures by the hundred and the record is complete. So far as [is] known no lives were taken by Knobbers in any save Taney and Christian counties.

In Christian county, the people who desired to improve the morals of their neighbors were first organized in September, 1885. Capt. Kinney went to all the counties adjoining Taney and made public addresses explaining the necessity of such an organization. In a speech at Sparta he denounced the officers of the law for failing to punish crime, then defied them and their friends to do him harm for his exposure of their weakness, and throwing open his coat and vest said dramatically, "Is anyone of them here that dare deny what I say? If so, let him emphasize his denial with a bullet through my heart!"

Ha! How those mountaineers went wild over that. Now that Kinney is dead, his friends deny that he was ever connected with any Knobbers outside of Taney.

The truth is, Kinney never actually initiated a member outside of Taney county; he merely prepared the war. The Christian county band was organized by Chief Joe Walker of Douglas county. Dave Walker, a brother of Joe, was made chief, and Dave's son, William, first lieutenant. The Rev. C.O. Simmons, a Baptist clergyman of excellent repute, was a charter member and one of the most active of Knobbers. He has since received a call to serve the Lord in another sphere. He obeyed the call promptly. Sheriff Johnson was the angel who bore it. Simmons is serving a twelve years' sentence for murder of the second degree.

The first job undertaken by them was the pouring out of John Rhoades's whiskey at Chadwick. Rhoades got a new supply, and under the direction of the Rev. Mr. Simmons this also was spilled, and Rhoades got a rope around his neck, but he was not hanged. Mrs. Rhoades was made to believe he would be, however, so as to frighten her. One other raid is worth detailing, because it was not wholly successful, and because the story of it and its results illustrate certain characteristics of the natives.

Over on Blue Ridge is a settlement known as the Swearingin settlement. Two brothers came there a long time ago, and raised two large families. From some cause the two families got to quarrelling, and a feud which, however, never resulted in murder was developed at about the time the Knobbers were organized. One family of Swearingin straightway joined the Knobbers. People here say this was the more respectable family. The other family became violent opponents of the Knobbers.

In the opposition family were Dodge and George and Bill, besides Beck McWilliams, a brother-in-law. One night the Knobbers started out to whip these four men "for indecency," the charge being undue familiarity with a widow and her two daughters, one of the daughters being an octoroon. It is admitted that the charge was true.

The Knobbers had their usual luck with three of the men. They were dragged out, tied up, and whipped soundly. The mob finally reached the house of Dodge just before daylight. This was an unfortunate hour for the mob. Dodge was an early riser. He was up and dressed and saw them coming. In spite of his immoral character, it must be said that Dodge had some very manly traits. He might have lawfully shot those men to death, and he had the tools to do it with, but he scorned to resort to firearms. Telling his wife not to be "skeered," he slipped out of the back door, got "a bit of a hickory" three or four feet long and an inch and a half thick, and hid in the scrub oaks handy nearby.

The mob took a big rail, and after getting a good ready rushed at the door, and down the door went. In an instant Dodge was among them, a welting every one in reach with his club. It was one against a dozen, but that one had the strength and courage of a modern Sampson, and although the rest were men of no mean strength and were as game as Dodge; yet the one cleaned out the dozen. He never could have done it, however; they would have downed and killed him soon had not the gray streak in the east been broadening into day so rapidly that they feared detection.

But they did not get off free after all. As they fled over the fence, Dodge noticed a dog belonging to one of them and caught it by the tail. After breakfast he put a rope on the dog and let it lead him to its home. It stopped at the home of Gill Applegate; it was Gill's dog.

Another of the assailants was Levi Swearingin, Dodge's own cousin. In the trial for assault that followed, Dodge and a neighbor swore that Levi must have been there, because at just the end of the time that it would take [a] man to go hurriedly from Dodge's to Levi's house they heard Levi's jackass bray in recognition of the approach of its master.

The jury convicted both Levi and Applegate without leaving their seats. Both were fined $100 and confined thirty days in jail. Applegate was convicted by his dog, Levi by his ass. The latter is said here to be the only case of its kind on record since the days of Balaam.

## 2

# WHIPPED BEFORE HE WAS MURDERED

In extension of the crime to be recorded in this chapter, the friends of the convicted say that the officers of the county secretly encouraged the Knobbers in their work. The ranch owners in Christian county had suffered pretty much from petty criminals. The Knobbers had frightened a good many petty criminals out of Taney county into Christian. Then the Christian county Knobbers made life a burden for a good many bad men and only a few good men. The ranch owners and wealthy citizens rejoiced when the bad men were whipped. As for those who were whipped unjustly, they were invariably poor in property. It was of little consequence. Besides, it was just a mistake at worst. "Go for 'em, Chief Dave! Good boy, Will!" That was the state of public sentiment.

A great many good citizens felt very solemn over the doings of the Knobbers, for Christian county contains many upright and intelligent people. What cared the Knobbers for these? Nothing. Knowing that more than 500 well-armed men belong[ed] to the order in Taney, 200 in Douglas, and 200 in Christian, and believing that every member would flock to their assistance in case they got into trouble, Dave Walker's band started out to paralyze the whole country.

The one crime on the Knobber calendar greater than all others was talking disrespectfully of the Knobbers. Men who merely refused to join them were not molested. Men who spoke of them as mistaken enthusiasts were tolerated. Here the line was drawn. Any stronger sort of disapproval called for a hickory rod. If then the Knobber would not bear adverse comment, what was his condition of mind when ridiculed?

An 1887 newspaper illustration of *A Whippin'*. *Library of Congress.*

Some time in the month of October, 1886, Will Edens, a young married man, industrious, honest, and in every way an exemplary citizen living on a farm three miles south of Sparta, shot a trespassing dog that was chasing his pigs. A day or two later, being in Sparta, he told about the dog, and described the beast. He was told that it belonged to John Mathews. Will said, "Huh! Reckon I done killed a Bald Knobber then."

Mathews was a known member of the order. The crowd laughed. It was simply meant as a joke, but it was the young man's death sentence practically. The laugh that followed rippled across the county. Every one repeated the joke, and every one not a Knobber laughed.

On the night after election in November a gang of Knobbers went to Edens' house, carrying a tie from the railroad near by. With that as a ram they burst open the door and dragged the young man out. He was asked what he had to say. He explained that he meant no harm or slur, and then denied that he had even said anything against the order, and asserted emphatically, "I can lick the man that told you gentlemen I ever done said it."

Then they tied him up and whipped him unmercifully. A young man named John Evans who was at the time helping Edens get out ties for the railroad, was whipped for being with Edens. Evans left the country [the] next day. Edens' young wife—she was only a girl of 16—begged him to go also, but Edens could not flunk. He said he had rather die than run.

Among the men who whipped Edens and Evans were Chief David Walker, Lieut. William Walker, John Mathews, Wiley Mathews, the Rev. Mr. Simmons, Bud Ray of Sparta, and a host of others. Bud Ray is mentioned because, although no one familiar with the case doubts his guilt of the blood of Evans at the subsequent murder, yet he came clear, and is now one of "Sparta's best citizens."

3

# THE MURDER OF EDENS AND GREEN

Will Edens lived on a homestead entered by his father, James Edens, a couple years before. The old man lived in a cabin on the westerly side of the railroad, three miles below Sparta, and Will lived sixty rods away, on the east side. Near the old man and his wife, Elizabeth, lived Charles Green, a young man who had married the old man's daughter Melvina. Green and his wife had two small children, the younger a baby three months old. Along in 1887, Melvina was taken with the measles and very nearly died. When at last she was convalescent she was carried over to her mother's, so that she and her children could be cared for more easily by her mother and Mrs. Will Edens. She was carried over there on March 10, which was also the birthday of Will Edens, and when the day was over the family passed the last pleasant night they will ever know.

The next night Friday, March 11, 1887, the Knobbers met in Smelter Hollow. The Hollow is a dark ravine a long way from any house, and just the place which a bloodthirsty novelist would select for the home of his villain. It was the regular place of rendezvous when any deviltry was on hand. The immediate object of the meeting that night was to consider the advisability of pouring out the whiskey which Buckeye Bill Roberts kept for sale over on Swan Creek. When the matter was brought up, Bud Ray and some others opposed it. This was novel, but the reason was that Uncle Sam Preston, a leading Knobber, had been indicted in the United States Court for intimidating witnesses in a moonshine case, and the friends of Preston thought that the Knobbers had better keep quiet until that case was settled, lest the prosecution, knowing that Preston was a Knobber, be enabled to bring up the unlawful Knobber deeds to prejudice the case.

The friends of Preston prevailed. Dave Walker then proposed that all go home down the creek in the ravine, as that was the nearer way. Will Walker and Wiley Mathews wanted to go by the county road. Both Will and Wiley were sulky. They "hated to be beat out of the fun," as they said.

The county road ran past the Edens homestead. Will and Wiley were determined to give young Edens another whipping for "his insolence in not leaving the country." At last Will Walker drew a long line in the sand along the creek, he said, "All that wants to go the ridge way step across that line."

A brush fire lighted the scene. Nearly all stepped over, and so all went the Ridge road. As they went along Will Walker stopped and cut a slender hickory gad just eight feet long.

It was nearly 11 o'clock when the Knobbers reached the vicinity of the Edens' homestead. They stopped to consult for a moment, and then the majority started across the field to Will Edens' house. They burst in the door, but found no one there. Will and his wife were sleeping over at the old man's house, in order that they might help take care of Will's sick sister, the wife of Charley Green.

The entire Eden family was sound asleep at the time. They had no dog to arouse them, and they did not even hear the crash when Will's door was knocked in. The first they knew a crowd of yelling demons was around the house shouting in spite of the presence of the Rev. C.O. Simmons. "Get up! Get out of there, —— you, or we will kill you!"

Will Edens and his wife slept on a shake-down beside the westerly door of the house, and beneath the only window. Will and his mother jumped out of bed at the same moment[,] the old lady grabbing a pistol from her husband's coat that hung above her head. Young Mrs. Edens followed, and then Charley Green, first reaching over to pat his wife's cheek and tell her not to be afraid, got out on the floor. Will said, "It's the Bald Knobbers after me again."

Drawing on his trousers, and at that moment, the firing began on the outside. Three guns were poked through the little window and discharged. By this time old Edens was up and taking the pistol from his wife.

At that moment both the westerly and the easterly doors were burst open with railroad ties. There was a light burning, and the Knobbers could see the interior plainly. They yelled at Will Edens, "Hold up yer hands,"

Will holding them up in plain view said, "They are up!"

"Hold 'em both up."

"They are both up!"

Another Knobber said, "Now pop it to him."

There was a roar of guns. Will shouted, "I'm shot!"

Will fell with a bullet through his face and neck.

Then the Knobbers rushed in, firing as they came. Charley Green was just straightening up from reassuring his wife when a revolver bullet crashed through his brains. The man who held the weapon turned to the sick woman on the bed: "Shet up yar damn head!"

It was young Will Walker who said it. She grabbed his mask and screamed the louder. Putting his pistol to her breast he pulled the trigger. At the same moment three men saw the old man with a pistol and jumped upon him. Though more than 50 years old, he threw one of them from his right arm, straightened it out, and pulled the trigger. Will Walker got the bullet in his right leg, and ran out bleating like a calf. Then the Knobber pushed the old man against the bed, pinning young Mrs. Edens beneath him, and while one hit him over the head with the edge of an axe, another shot him through the neck.

Drenched in the blood that spurted from her father-in-law's wounds, young Mrs. Edens slipped from beneath him and ran to her husband, taking his head in her lap. The boy's mother was on her knees beside him, swaying her body from side to side and praying aloud to God for help.

Supposing the men dead, the Knobbers slipped out. Will was gasping. His wife got up to go for water, leaving him partly up on his elbow.

Standing just outside the door was Willy Mathews. He saw that Will was still alive, and raising his gun he shot the wounded man in the side. Buckshot pierced Will's heart and lungs. Then the Knobbers rode away.

Mrs. Green had escaped death by throwing young Walker's pistol up just as he pulled the trigger. She had the end of her right forefinger shot off, though. Old Mr. Edens recovered, of a strong constitution.

From the testimony of those who were there that night, the chief concern of the Knobbers as they left the house was the care of wounded Will Walker. As to their own safety, Chief Dave Walker told each what he was to say in case of arrest, and all sworn to obey, in order that their stories would agree. Charles Graves says he, Inman, McGuire, and Applegate were told to swear they were all playing cards at Inman's that night.

# 4
# THE CIVIL AUTHORITIES INTERESTED AT LAST

That Capt. Kinney should have died from a pistol-shot wound precisely like the wound he inflicted on young Andrew Coggburn was poetic justice. That David Walker and his son William and John Mathews and his nephew Wiley, the Christian county leaders, should die on the lawful gallows, as they are likely to do, is justice of the sort that terrifies evil doers.

The three women in the Edens household were left alone with the dead save only for the arrival of Charley Green's father, who lived near, and came over after the Knobbers left until 9 o'clock the next morning. They simply sat on the floor, each by her own husband, and wept and prayed the night away. The neighbors did not dare go near them until long after daylight.

Finally old man Green went to Sparta and told the gruesome story. It spread over the village like a flash, but it was not until 8 o'clock that a crowd of thirty or forty collected and started for the scene. Not one of Sparta's physicians dared go to care for the wounded.

The citizens reached the house at 9 o'clock. The men all lay as they fell. The women still sat on the floor beside them. The floor was covered with blood; the table, the beds, the walls, and the ceiling were blotched and spattered with it. Pieces of broken chairs and dishes were scattered about with the splintered remnants of the doors. A more horrifying picture those people never saw.

The old man was manifestly alive, and he was lifted to a bed and his wounds washed so that he gained consciousness. The bodies of the two young men were carried out and laid on the floor of a rough porch on the easterly side of the house, and were prepared for the grave. Jeweller T.C. Adams of Sparta measured the bodies so that coffins could be ordered, using the hickory gad that Will Walker had cut. It was the last whip ever cut by the Bald Knobbers.

Justice of the Peace J.N. Adams impaneled a jury, and they brought in the verdict customary among jurors willfully ignorant: "Died of gunshot wounds at the hands of men to the jury unknown." There were Knobbers on the jury.

The next day, Sunday, Elder Bird of the Baptist Church preached a funeral sermon that was not worded to roil the Bald Knobbers, and the bodies were buried in the Sparta Cemetery.

More than 2,000 people attended the funeral, and more than 5,000 visited the wrecked home within those two days. Men had been murdered in the county before, but not since the war had there been so much excitement. Men who had laughed at the whipping of the "trifling creatures" called for vengeance when two hard-working, reputable citizens were murdered for no greater offense than "talkin'." Green had not even talked.

Prosecuting Attorney G.A. Watson was promptly on hand the day after the murder, and with Deputy Sheriff Miller (the Sheriff being out of the county) began an investigation. Mrs. Melvina Green was taken before Justice Sloan of Ozark and warrants were sworn out for men on information and belief. The first Knobber arrested was old Sam Preston, whose case before the United States Court prevented the attack on Buckeye Bill Roberts that night. He was taking the railcars to flee the county. He was not in the murder, they say, but he knew things that helped implicate the real murderers, and he gave the things away to save himself. Bud Ray, young Sam Preston, and Jim Preston were arrested on Monday. These three gave things away, too. The Rev. Mr. Simmons, with shirt sleeves spotted with blood, was taken in among the rest. Sheriff Johnson got home on Monday and swore in six deputies, who, with him and Deputy Miller, scoured the country. The prisoners were confined on the upper floor of the Ozark Court House.

It was a time of wild excitement in this village at that time. A raid, headed by Capt. Kinney in person, was expected by prisoners and people alike. Capt C.O. Hill was elected commander of the home guard that was organized, and every night 100 armed citizens patrolled the streets. The Captain himself, expecting a double share of Knobber vengeance for leading the home guard, mined his yard about his home with gun cotton and connected it with an electric battery, so that, should he be attacked, he had only to touch a button and blow the smithereens out of the mob.

The mines are kept in working order to this day, for no one believes here that the trouble is over.

It is an interesting but unpleasant fact for the Ozark people, that at the height of excitement—a young couple were married. Some boys started in to "bell" them, and the racket all but drove the citizens wild. They thought the Knobbers were upon them. One prominent merchant ran home from his store, picked wife and children out of bed, bundled them up in blankets, and ran out of town with them. Capt. Hill suppressed the belling.

A special term of court was held to dispose of the Knobber cases. Three hundred indictments were found, and nearly 300 arrests made. Indictments for assault and battery, unlawfully assembling, and riot were found against 145 men for the various whippings. Of these 103 have either pleaded guilty or have been convicted. The fines averaged $10 each, and thirty-eight were imprisoned for want of the money, besides others who were imprisoned and fined both.

Sixteen were indicted for murder in the first degree for killing Charley Green, as follows: David Walker, William Walker, John Mathews, Wiley Mathews, James Mathews, William Stanley, Amos Jones, C.O. Simmons, Joseph Inman, Charlie Graves, Joseph Hyde, Lewis Davis, William Newton, Peter Davis, Andrew Adams, and Gilbert Applegate. All these, save Lewis Davis, were also indicted for killing Edens. All were arrested save Will Walker. For a long time he could not be located. The story of his capture is worth noting.

# 5

# JOE INMAN CONFESSES

## Shot Down Out of Sport

March 16, 1887.—Taney, Ozark, Christian, and Douglas counties in the extreme southern portion of Missouri, west of the centre of the State, sparsely settled, and until recently devoid of railroad communication with the outside world, have for months been dominated by an oath bound combination laying claim to be law and order men, but as appears, degenerated into a mere lawless mob, more to be dreaded than the worst outlaws.

The inception of the organization grew out of the reckless defiance of law by the older settlers and their descendants, and the laxity with which the law was enforced. One of the desperados named Layton, shot and killed a Forsyth man named Everett, who was unarmed, and who was well liked in the community. Layton was arrested, but trial was a farce by reason of the drunken condition of the jury, who were freely supplied with whiskey during the trial by the friends of the prisoner. Layton's acquittal by the drunken jury aroused the more orderly class of the community, and, at the insistence of the murdered man's brother, an organization was at once effected. Very soon others of the better class of citizens heard of the movement and expressed their desire to join. It is asserted that the organization extends not merely throughout southwestern Missouri, but into Arkansas, Texas, Indian Territory and Kansas.

Naturally, with its prodigious growth, the order has absorbed other classes than those of which it was originally composed, and the lawless have found opportunity to creep into it in such numbers as to destroy its original character and reverse its purposes. Their sway culminated a couple weeks ago in a midnight raid upon the families of Charles Green and Charles Eaton Jr., near Sparta, in Christian county.

This tragedy spurred the law officers of Christian county to a sense of their duty, and a raid in turn was made on the outlaws, which has resulted in the capture of a dozen of the ringleaders who are now confined in the jail at this place. One of the number has made a full confession and has been taken to Springfield for safety. Among the members of the organization are men of all sorts—farmers, preachers, saloon keepers, loafers, and so on. The confession of Joe Inman gives the first clear story of the specific crime for which those arrests were made.

Inman says that on Friday night, the 11$^{th}$ inst., the Bald Knob Company to which he belonged commanded by "Chief of Bull Creek" Dave Walker, met at the old smelter on Bull Creek for the purpose of going down to Chadwick to pour some whiskey kept by "Bucky Bill Roberts." There were some thirty of the band, about one half of whom were mounted, the others being on foot. After going some distance, it was decided that the trip would be to laborious for the footmen, and Chief Walker told the latter they might go home, while he and his mounted Knobbers would ride down and dispose of the whiskey.

At about this time, they came in sight of Eden's house which was near the railroad on which the unmounted members of the band were walking. Some of the younger Knobbers proposed to go down to the house and have some fun. The chief, Walker, he says, protested against this movement, but the reckless boys started at once on a full run toward the house. Inman says he remained on the railroad till the party reached the house. As soon as the Knobbers got to the house they knocked both doors down, when old Mr. Eden fired at the crowd and shot young Bill Walker in the groin. The Knobbers then returned the fire and did the fatal work, which left the house a scene of slaughter. When the firing began, he and the rest of the party that had stopped on the railroad, ran down to the house and tried to stop the massacre.

Inman says the men who first ran down to the house and did the shooting were young Bill Walker, assistant chief of the band; Wiley, John and Jim Mathews; C.O. Simmons; Amos Jones; Will Newton; Jack and Andy Hiles; and probably Joe Hyde. He says the chief, Dave Walker, did all he could to prevent both the attack on the house and the subsequent firing. Young Bill Walker was, he says, fatally shot as he saw him lie down in the yard and pull off his mask, which was left on the ground.

Inman did not know, he says, that anybody was killed. He thought some of the family was hurt from the cries he heard. About ten shots were fired he thinks. As soon as the shooting was over, the Knob party left the house. Dave Walker, chief, was assisting his wounded son in getting away. When they had gone a short distance, Chief Walker told him and some other Knobbers to go back and get his son's gun and mask, which they refused to do. He says he knows the boys had no thought of serious trouble when they started to the house, and only meant to have a little Bald Knob sport. As soon as this confession was made, the Sheriff went at once to the court room and handcuffed the persons most seriously criminated by Inman.

The members of the gang who have been arrested, and their occupations so far as known are as follows:

Sam Preston Sr., aged 54, married
Sam Preston Jr., son of former, aged 26, married
James Preston, aged 23 married, farmer
Bud Ray, aged 28, married, farmer
William Roberts, aged 37, married, farmer
Joe Hyde, aged 25, married, member of the Christian Church and teacher
C.O. Simmons, aged 35, married, Baptist preacher
Dave Walker, age 45, married, member of the Baptist church
Charlie Graves, aged 35, formerly a merchant and saloon keeper of Chadwick
William Abbott, age 44, married, farmer, a member of the Baptist church
John Mathews, age 38, married, farmer
Wiley Mathews, aged 26, married, farmer
Amos Jones, aged 19, unmarried
Joe Inman, aged 30, married
Wilson Stanley, aged 26, married
William Newton, aged 25, unmarried

The Knobbers last arrested have not been allowed to see the three Prestons, Ray, and Roberts, who were arrested previously. Some of the prisoners were very much dejected, and refuse to talk about anything, while others are quite communicative, and considering the grave charge under which they are held, were very cheerful [in] appearance. They all protest their innocence of any connection with the massacre of the 11th, and also disavow the slightest knowledge of the inside character of the Bald Knobbers' organization. It is confidently believed by the officers and the best-informed citizens here that the Bald Knobbers' conspiracy of Christian county will be thoroughly broken up by the trial of those prisoners, and that almost all the parties concerned in the killing of Eaton and Green are now in the Court House gloomily meditating on that cowardly crime, and the prospect of inevitable punishment through a vigorous enforcement of the law. The officers know much that cannot yet be made public, but they do not hesitate to say that a clue has been discovered which will lend to a thorough and irresistible disclosure of not only the persons involved in the murder of Eaton and Green, but also the whole dark history of Bald Knob lawlessness in Christian county.

Joe Inman whose confession is given above says:

> *It's a heap bigger thing than most people have any idea of, and the members of the Bald Knob gang are more desperate and powerful than is supposed. Why, there are 800 in Christian county, and there are members even in Springfield. I was taken out, a rope put around my neck, and told I would be hung if I didn't.*

Deputy Sheriff Neville says that pickets are stationed half a mile from Ozark in every direction, and no one can pass in or out without giving the countersign. He forgot it himself once, was halted by five armed men, and had great difficulty in getting through.

Preacher C.O. Simmons, Joseph Hyde, two of the Mathews boys, and two Hiles were placed in irons. They were almost overcome with horror when this new development took place, and knew, no doubt, that Inman had betrayed them.

Simmons sent for a newspaper man, and the only request he had to make was that he might be furnished with a small Testament that he could hold in his manacled hand. He said that he did not know that he could get any comfort from the Word of God, however, with those horrid things on. A small copy of the New Testament was found and sent as a present to the terror-stricken preacher whose face was indeed a pitiable index of mental torture. Hyde's expression after being handcuffed was also livid and horrible. The rest of the ironed Knobbers were very gloomy, but did not so completely break down.

Inman says the three Prestons, Ray and Roberts, the five first arrested, were not connected with the raid, though all active Bald Knobbers. He says he joined the organization under protest, being forced at the muzzle of a shotgun, with a rope around his neck, to swear allegiance to the deadly fraternity. This, he says, is the way many were taken into the organization

He had, he says, admitted to the chief of the band that the pouring out of the whiskey at Chadwick last summer was a good thing. Soon after, he was invited out on a night and initiated in the order in the prescribed manner. He says that once in the organization there is no getting out, as any betrayal of the secrets is certain death.

He says he wanted to be out of the order from the night he was forced to join it, but dared not attempt to free himself from his terrible oath. He states that he many times feigned sickness to avoid going out with the band and has more than once been warned to take a more active part in the nightly operations of the masked outlaws. Fully three fourths of the men in the eastern part [of the] county, he says, belong to the order.

They always told him the object of the organization was to put down crimes such as the civil law could not suppress: selling whiskey, keeping loose women &c. Inman begged to be taken to Springfield after making his confession, as he said his life would pay the forfeit of his treachery if the Bald Knobbers could get to him. He would not think of staying with his late confederates in the Court House, though armed men were inside as guards. He was accordingly taken to the Springfield jail by J.H. Neville this afternoon on the 3 o'clock train. Inman's confession has produced the most intense excitement here and rumors are again rife of a contemplated attempt on the part of the Bald Knobbers of Christian, Taney and Douglas counties to release the prisoners. People here think this is a groundless sensation. The law and order sentiment is now on top and means to hold the vantage at all hazards. It is said there are 930 Bald Knobbers in Taney county, and probably as many more in Douglas.

Young Walker, the young outlaw who was shot by the Edens, has not been seen since the night of that raid, and he is believed to have died, but different members of his family give statements as to his whereabouts—one saying that he went away from home a month ago, others that he left last Sunday. His father says that he is in Pierce City, and his mother says he is elsewhere. It is believed he may be hiding in the woods about three miles from Chadwick. The gun left in Eaton's house has been examined by several persons who say there is no doubt that it belongs to young Walker, as it is peculiarly made and easily identified.

# 6

# MATHEWS CONFESSES TO THE BUTCHERY

March 17, 1888.—The Trial of The Bald Knobbers at Ozark was interrupted yesterday by the breaking down of John Mathews, whose case was called at 1 o'clock. The prisoner appeared to be in a despairing condition and one presented the Prosecuting Attorney a paper, which was at once handed back to him. He then handed it to the Judge, who returned it with the instructions to first submit it to his attorney. He was evidently desirous of making confession to any person who would listen to him. Mathews confessed to a liberal share of the Edens-Green butchery. He says it was a blow from his Winchester rifle, and not from an ax, that knocked old man Edens senseless.

An 1889 newspaper illustration of John Mathews. *Library of Congress.*

Bill Walker shot Charley Green through the temple with a pistol while the young man was held by another Knobber. Wiley Mathews, the defendant's nephew, shot Bill Edens in the back with a load of buckshot. The statement exculpates Graves. John Mathews, the broken-hearted man, said, "I want to tell all I did in that thing and take my punishment. I don't want any trial. I came here this evening to tell all I know and take my sentence to the pen. I was [led] to that thing; I don't think I am guilty of murder in the first degree."

A motion for a change of venue was received.

7

# REV. C.O. SIMMONS

## Grieved in Spirit

March 18, 1887.—All fears of an attack from the Bald Knobbers have subsided. The general feeling is that officers, supported by the law abiding citizens, are masters of the situation. Sheriff Johnson and Almus Harrington returned from Chadwick yesterday afternoon, bringing five more Bald Knobbers charged with being implicated in the murder of Green and Edens Friday night. Their names are Andres Adams, J.W. Robinson, Lew and Pete Davis and Gil Applegate. Jim McGuire was also arrested and brought in on horseback making the twenty-fifth man now under arrest. Most of the prisoners are handcuffed together in couples or manacled at the ankles and kept under strong guard at the court house. All still protest their innocence, notwithstanding the confession made by Joe Inman. They appear by no means cheerful, however, are quite cautious in what they have to say. Their vocation is farming, and nearly all have lived in this part of the state for many years.

C.O. Simmons, who was ordained as a Baptist preacher three years ago, is perhaps an average lot in intelligence and education. He is thirty years old and has a wife and three children, and combines preaching and farming. When asked if he had any thing to say to the public, through the press, he handed the following, which is given verbatim [et] literatim:

> *Ozark, Mo., March 17, 1887.—I feel a few lines would ad some thing to your paper. It looks hard that Honest men has got to be cathalled in this way while they have to, toil all day for support for their family and then*

## GRIEVED IN SPIRIT.

### Rev. C. O. Simmons, the Bald Knobber, Very Much Hurt By Being

Manacled to a Companion, But He Remembers Paul—A Characteristic Letter.

An 1887 newspaper title: "Grieved in Spirit." *Library of Congress.*

*lay down at night to rest from the hard days toil. Some night prowler will get out an commit such bloody deeds an ennocent men has to suffer for it. I want to say this to the people that the god of heaven noes who done that bloody deed and he noes that I, C.O. Simmons, is more ennocent of that crime than Pilate was of the blood of our savier but there is one thing that is a consolation to me and that is Christ says that he will never forsake his people. Though all men may cast your name out as evil yet I will never forsake you. I know that men around Ozark would hang me if they daire, but good lord is able and will take care of his people. The apostle Pal was put in prison and prayer was made without crying for him and the holy spirit was all his comfort. So it is mine while in this horrible condition I no that I have friends that is sending petitions to a throne of grase. In behalf. Among them is my old mother and dar companion and two darling girls and plenty of brothers and sisters in Christ Jesus.*
*C.O. SIMMONS*

Rev. Simmons was handcuffed to A.J. Hiles, a young man, and appeared very much grieved in spirit over his unpleasant surroundings. "Bullock Dave" Walker, the alleged chief of the company, who committed the murder, denounced Inman's statement as false, and declared that he had never attended a meeting of the Bald Knobbers or been connected with the organization in any manner. He said he had never seen a Bald Knobber to his knowledge except Captain Kinney, the reputed chief of the Taney County companies.

William Walker, the young man who was wounded, has not yet been found, and it is surmised by some that he died the same night and his body was hidden by other members of the company. His father claims that he is in Pierce City. The gun found at the Edens['] house after the murder, however has been positively identified as the one kept by him, and which corroborates Inman's statement. The prosecution feels assured they have the guilty parties, as well as ample evidence to secure their conviction although other clues are being followed up and still further developments are anticipated.

## 8

## LURED BY HIS SWEETHEART

April 1, 1887.—The officers were particularly anxious to capture young Will Walker. Not only was he a principal, as they quickly learned, but it was hurtful to their pride to have a wounded man escape. So Sheriff Johnson and Assistant Prosecutor Herrington—commonly called "Babe"—put their heads together and resolved to locate Walker through his sweetheart.

The girl was a mountain lass of sixteen. Her name was Lois Newton. She was the sister of William Newton, who was indicted for the murder. Will Walker was "head over heels" in love with her, but she "only jest smooched him fer fun," to use the local vernacular. She very readily agreed to capture Will, on condition that her brother William's neck should be saved. Her brother Joseph came into the agreement on the same terms. Will Newton was about as bad as anyone; it was he who held Old Edens' arm while Dave Walker hit the old man on the head with an axe and John Mathews shot him through the neck. But it was necessary to let some go partly free in order to get witnesses for the State.

Accordingly, Miss Lois became greatly grieved because she could not see her wounded sweetheart, and nothing would do but she must go to him. Her mother, innocent soul, not knowing her daughter's guile, tried to talk her out of it, but Joe said it was all right. He would hitch up and take her. The Walkers fell into the trap at once, and told the girl that Will was at John Walker's in Baxter county, Arkansas.

People are somewhat bad down that way. Sheriff Johnson wanted to get Walker to a railway station, so the girl and her brother were sent to West

An 1889 newspaper illustration of William "Will" Walker. *Library of Congress.*

Plains in Howell county, and thence the brother went down into Baxter and met Will.

It tickled Will Walker literally to death to learn that his sweetheart had come as far as West Plains to see him—that is, it will be literally to death if he hangs in consequence of his capture and although very lame from his wound, he hastened over to West Plains, Sheriff Johnson and another met him there. Sheriff Johnson explained, "He made a motion to get his revolver. But I poked my revolver right in his face and told him to throw up his hands, and he did throw them up."

The young man missed seeing his girl entirely. He doesn't want to see her now.

# 9
# CHARLIE GRAVES MAKES A CLEAN BREAST

April 20, 1888.—The Bald Knobber situation opened quietly this morning, and remained rather tame till about noon, when it became known that Charley Graves had entered the confessional and was making a clean breast of all he knew concerning the Edens-Green murder and the other nightly operations of the masked regulators. This morning at 8 o'clock Graves was quietly removed from the court-room and taken to E.O. Hill's law office, where, in the presence of the former gentlemen, Prosecuting Attorney G.A. Watson, Sheriff Z.A. Johnson, Deputy W.H.H. Miller and Almus Harrington, he began his lengthy story. From 8 o'clock till 3 in the afternoon the prisoner continued to unload his burdened memory, detailing the history of the last bloody act in the drama of the Christian County Bald Knobism, and then going over the whole series of minor depredations about Chadwick and Sparta, of which he had any knowledge.

### DETAILS OF THE CONFESSION

The full details of Grave's confession are not accessible, but the *GLOBE-DEMOCRAT* representative obtained some hints from parties present that indicate the general scope of his story. He was not at the house when the assault was made on the Edens-Green family, but heard some statements from active participants in the massacre after the band started home, which are most damaging facts yet developed. According to the testimony of Mrs. Edens, her son George was shot down in the first assault on the family, immediately after the doors of the house were broken in and the masked assailants rushed into the cabin. Her son was lying on the floor when the Knobbers went out of the house and not dead, but able to raise his head and rest it on his elbow. She was by the wounded man's side and trying to protect him from further harm. The marauders consulted some time in the yard, she says, and one man came to the door, deliberately aimed a shotgun at her prostrate son's head and fired, instantly killing him. Mrs. Edens has told this story in the same way from the beginning, and all the prisoners who have made confessions corroborate the woman's statement with regard to the fact that a solitary shot was fired some time after the first attack. Mrs. Edens says it was several minutes after the main assault was over when this masked man came back to the door of the house and fired the final shot which killed her son. The witness who stood on the railroad and took no part in the assault, according to their own story, did not make the interval between the general volley and the last shot so long as two or three minutes, but they all say it was fired after the attack seemed to be over.

## George Edens' Slayer

Now it is learned that Graves has told who fired this last shot and killed George Edens. He says after the attacking party left the house and joined him and the party on the railroad, John Mathews, who was bleeding from a slight wound in the back of the head, admitted he fired this last shot and ended the life of young Edens. Mathews said his wound in the head made him so mad that he determined to finish the work begun on George Edens, and went back and fired the fatal shot. If this part of Grave's confession is correctly reported, and his evidences receive any credence in court, John Mathews will doubtless rank chief himself in sharing guilt of the band. Graves went with the party over a mile down the railroad, after the killing, and heard more guilty parties talk freely when the Bald Knobbers' oath of secrecy was still thought to be inviolable. His confession covers specifically a number of other night raids about Chadwick during summer and fall when the Bald Knobbers were making their first record by wearing out so many Bull Creek switches and spilling contraband whisky. He knows a great deal about these earlier depredations, and seems to have been a very active member of the Chadwick company, the oldest Bald Knobber organization in Christian County.

## Other Confessions Offered

Graves' is the fullest history of the Bald Knob movement in this country yet given from behind the mask, and if his evidence receives much weight when he goes before the Grand Jury, it will likely be the foundation for a number of indictments outside of the Edens-Green case. One of the Graves' said that Parson Simmons and Will Newton were both anxious to get into the confessional, if a full statement of what they know would be of any advantage to them in mitigating the rigor of the law, but the State has now all the evidence necessary, the Prosecuting Attorney thinks, and further confessions will not be sought by any promise of mercy.

## The Prisoners Despondent

The prisoners are very much broken down this evening. They have lost the spirit that animated them yesterday, and even Walker and his son show strong signs of deep dejection. They have spent much of the day in consulting their attorneys. F.M. Wolf and O.H. Travers have come down from Springfield and will shield, as far as their legal ability can avail, nine of the Knobbers. Wolf represents Andy Adams and his son. Senator J.J. Gideon is on the scene of action, but has made no definite engagements yet. He has been consulted by a number of the prisoners, but has declined the fees offered.

## Dave Walker's War Record

Mr. Gideon served through the war with Dave Walker, in Company H, Sixteenth Missouri Calvary, and says no braver man ever faced danger of the battlefield than the late reputed chief of the Bald Knob clan. In testimony of his military service, the central figure of the Bald Knob prisoners now wears on his breast a Grand Army badge. A former companion-in-arms remarked during the conversation, "Dave Walker would fight a whole regiment single-handed."

Thirty witnesses have already been summoned to appear before the Grand Jury, and the Sheriff says the list will be increased before the investigation is through. A young Applegate, son of one of the prisoners, presented to Sheriff Johnson this evening a written request for the pistols taken from Jesse

Robertson at the time of his arrest, the note stating the undersigned had bought the weapons, but the officer refused to surrender the property. No indictments have been returned to-day. A strong guard is in the room with the prisoners, and a reserve force in the hall outside.

 The Bald Knob prisoners are gaining confidence as Graves and Inman have become terrified that their confessions did not relieve them from indictment. Jack Hiles has become convinced of the enormity of the crimes committed, and made a clean breast of his part of the raid, giving the names of 200 members of the organization and relating particulars of the descent, on E.P. Helms and the destruction of John P. Hodes' whisky shops. Graves has agreed to take the sheriff to the place where the Bald Knobbers' masks and arms are concealed. The Grand Jury will report fourteen more indictments for murder in the first degree for the killing of William Green.

## 10

# THE BLESSINGS OF LIBERTY— FROM JAIL

July 11, 1887.—The G.A.R. Post at Sparta has received a letter from Bald Knobber Chief, Davis Walker, written in the Springfield Jail on the Fourth of July, which is having a very extensive reading in the eastern section of Christian County. Walker was a member of the Sparta Post, and wears now in his prison cell the regulation badge of the military order. The chief's Fourth of July letter covers four pages of paper, and while spelling shows many deviations from the prevailing usages of English orthography, the composition is reasonably good and the thought and sentiment expressed would be creditable any where.

The theme of the letter is the boon of liberty, and while the writer does not directly refer to his own condition, the prisoner's sigh may be heard in the general tone of the epistle. The Knobber chief begs his neighbors and old companions in arms to appreciate properly the blessings of liberty which they are permitted to enjoy, and reminds them of the great sacrifices that our forefathers made in order to transmit to the present generation the day of Independence. How much the now noted leader of the Christian regulators longed for freedom of his native hills as he penned these words in one of the most loathsome prisons in the civilized world, can perhaps be only faintly imagined. Dave Walker never before knew the chafing restraint of prison bars. He has always lived an active life and this sudden change from woodland freedom of the tie cutter to the dark and noisome cell of the Springfield Jail must try most severely the stubborn spirit of the Chadwick Bald Knobber chief.

An 1889 newspaper illustration of David Walker, "Bull Creek Dave." *Library of Congress.*

Walker's letter will be passed around among that large circle of persons in Christian County who, either through Bald Knob sympathy or mere curiosity, take a deep interest in all that in any way relates to this famous prisoner, and it may be safely predicted that before the August term of court few people from Ozark and Swan Creek will not be familiar with its contents.

## 11

# BALD KNOBBER PRISONERS & CRAZED WIFE

August 22, 1887.—The Bald Knobbers are again in Ozark, occupying now Christian County's new jail instead of the Court House, where they were quartered last spring. It had been understood throughout the country that the prisoners would not be brought down from Springfield until to-day. And more than 1,000 people were expecting to be in Ozark this morning in time to see the Knobbers and witness also the dedication of the new jail, but Sheriff Johnson, wishing to avoid the immense crowd that he knew would be in town to-day, stole a march on the thousand people of Christian County who were eagerly anticipating of the approaching Monday by quietly taking the train for Springfield, accompanied by two trusty deputies, and returned Sunday morning with the prisoners. Only a few people in Ozark knew of the Sheriff's movements until Sunday morning, and the entire county remained in ignorance of the affair till the Knobbers were lodged in the Ozark Jail. Before train time Sunday morning the secret was generally known. When the train drew up at the station the portly form of Sheriff Johnson stepped down from the cars, followed by Walker and band.

### Handcuffed in Pairs

All were handcuffed in pairs, except Joe Inman and Charley Graves, who brought up the rear of the procession unchained. This little boon of freedom enjoyed by Inman and Graves is the reward of that voluminous confession made by these two Knobbers last spring, in which the whole secret of the Edens-Green massacre was completely given away. The prisoners looked much better, as a rule, than could have been expected of men taken from an active life and confined six months in such a place as the Greene County Jail as is now known to be. Though all the men were much whitened by their confinement in the dark cells of that noisome prison, but two or three showed and marked signs of physical or mental injury. David Walker had the same firm and resolute bearing that characterized the Knobber chief last spring when the band were first arrested.

William Walker, the son of the chief, and second officer of the Chadwick company, was improved very much in appearance since his committal to jail, as at the time he was suffering from the wound received in the thigh the night of the fatal raid. He has fully recovered, and shows every feature of his youthful face the strong, dauntless character that made him his father's first and most trusted lieutenant during the reign of the Bald Knobbers' terror in Christian County.

C.O. Simmons is about the healthiest looking man of the band. The parson's ruddy face has undergone but little change during his summer's confinement, and prison life seems to have borne almost as lightly upon the Baptist minister as would the exercise of two weeks' religious revival. Andy Adams, who, twelve months ago, was one of the most industrious and prosperous farmers of Swan Creek has suffered.

## Glad of a Change

The prisoners were all delighted with the prospect of a new situation in the Ozark Jail, where they could see their friends. They all carried in their hands a bundle of clothes, and had washed and dressed to go home, as they called the Ozark Jail. As the procession marched up from the depot to the jail the Knobbers talked eagerly to the crowd that followed along, and all of them seemed to be in the best of spirits. At 11:30 o'clock the prisoners were taken into the jail and unchained, being allowed the freedom of the corridors till night. The Sheriff soon brought the prisoners a good dinner which was eaten with the keenest of relish.

In the afternoon some of the families of the prisoners came into town to be ready for court, and were surprised to find their Knobber friends already in jail. Among the arrivals were wife and children of William Stanley, wife and mother of Parson Simmons, and wife and children of John Mathews, besides numerous male relations of the other Knobbers. The wagons containing these families stopped in front of the jail, and as soon as the children learned that the absent dear ones of their homes were inside the prison walls, a most pathetic scene followed. The little boys and girls, ranging from age 6 to 12 years, jumped out of the wagon, ran to the jail and climbed up the grated window to peep through and get a sight of their fathers within. Though several feet intervened between the children and their imprisoned friends, and two sets of steel bars prevented, for a time, a nearer approach, the meeting was happy and touching.

## Talking Through the Bars

The little ones talked eagerly to fathers and brothers whose caresses they could not yet enjoy, and told them much that happened at home during the long separation that to children's minds must have seemed an age. Soon the Sheriff allowed the wives of the prisoners to go into the jail and see their husbands a few minutes. The faithful had brought bundles of clothes, apples, home-cooked delicacies and tobacco, which were distributed among the rightful owners of those evidences of wifely devotion. After coming out of the jail the women and children got into the wagons and drove out to a common adjoining the town, where they went into camp, having brought a supply of provisions along, expecting to remain near their friends several days. After the prisoners had their supper, they began to sing some familiar revival songs, until 10 o'clock the jail resounded with the voices of the entire band. Parson Simmons' strong, melodious voice could be clearly distinguished leading the prison choir, and the words of the hymns, "Ninety and Nine," and "Oh, How I love Jesus," and several other big meeting songs often heard in Christian County during the revival season of the year, rang out clearly on the still air of the sultry August night.

During the night a guard was kept on duty around the jail, but nothing occurred to excite alarm. By daylight the rain was pouring down in a steady torrent, and the camp-fires could hardly be kept from going out while friends of the prisoners cooked their breakfast. On account of the rain, the crowd was later coming in than was expected, and many were no doubt kept away by the unfavorable weather.

# Bald Knobbers

## Crowds of Spectators

Before noon, however, the Court-house yard and the ground around the jail were covered with men from all parts of the county, making the largest crowd that ever attended Circuit Court at Ozark. Wagon-load after wagon-load of relatives and friends of prisoners kept coming in. By noon the ropes stretched around the jail to prevent the near approach of the crowd were lined with women and children, who talked constantly to husbands, fathers and brothers behind prison-bars. Melons were brought by the wagon-load by sympathetic spectators and sent to the Knobbers by the Sheriff and his deputies. The whole regulating order of Christian County, who had worn the black mask with Chief Walker and his prison companions on various nightly raids; were in town by this time, and the ex-Knobbers around the jail exchanged many lively jokes with old associates.

Judge Hubbard opened court at 1 o'clock, the court-room being packed to its utmost capacity, while hundreds of men outside could not get a peep at the scene within, while his Honor instructed the Grand Jury. The Judge reproduced much of his charge to the special Grand Jury last spring, when the Bald Knobbers were first brought under the jurisdiction of a court of law, and told the twelve men that they had a better opportunity to investigate the

An 1889 newspaper illustration of "Courthouse in Ozark, Missouri." *Library of Congress.*

acts of the Christian County regulators than the former inquiring tribunal possessed, as the backbone. The jury are all good, substantial citizens, not one of whom has the slightest Bald Knobber sympathies.

Several motions to quash some of the minor Bald Knob indictments were held. Two of these motions were in favor of John and William Mapes, sons of Parson H.J. Mapes, who were indicted for perjury by the special Grand Jury. These young men absolved themselves from the obligation of the Bald Knob oath when they went before that body to testify in regard to their knowledge of the regulating order.

## A Shocking Scene

At 4 o'clock, while the court was in session there occurred at the jail a scene of horror that baffles description. The wives and children were assembled in front of a vacant house about 40 yards south of the jail, where they could be seen by the prisoners, the wife of William Stanley had a severe chill in the morning, and when the fever came on she fell into a sound sleep. From this troubled slumber the sick woman awoke in the wildest frenzy. All at once the frantic shrieks of the poor woman were heard in every-part of town as she ran toward the jail with both hands raised above her head, praying toward heaven to protect and save her imprisoned husband, she passed under the ropes that surrounded the jail without stopping and ran to the prison window nearest her husband, seizing the iron grating with all the energy of madness. She told her husband that for six months she had prayed day and night for his deliverance, and she believed her petitions would open the prison doors before morning. Her cries were taken up by other women, and the children, frightened at this strange and terrible scene, screamed at the top of their voices.

## An Excited Crowd

The crowd gathered around the excited woman, men rushing out of the court-room in a panic to see what was the matter, until one dense mass of human beings surged in front of the jail, gazing awe-stricken on the tragic spectacle. The prisoners wept like children and tears streamed down the faces of strong men in the crowd without. It was universally pronounced the saddest scene ever witnessed here. A great many people believed that grief had suddenly crazed the poor woman, few knowing she had a fever. She would not be quieted and refused to leave the jail for several minutes, continuing to exhort the crowd in the most fevered manner. She said she was not crazy though people would call her so. She told her husband and his fellow prisoners to stand firm and the Lord would vindicate the innocent, and for more than an hour poured forth the fullness of her troubled heart and fevered brain. Language can not paint the wild grief which this novel event produced, and its like will never probably be witnessed again.

Parson Simmons sent to-day one of the Springfield papers a card of thanks to the Christian ladies of the city who visited the jail and ministered to the wants of himself and his fellow prisoners during their confinement there. The preacher, on behalf of the prisoners, also thanks Deputy Sheriff's Hindman and Green for their kindness.

Just before court adjourned John Wilson threw himself upon the mercy of the Judge and pleaded guilty to the indictment for whipping Green Walker last October. The Court took the case under consideration and will not assess the fine till Saturday. As this is the first plea of guilty for a Bald Knob assault, and there are about ninety-five similar charges pending, the decision of the Court will be looked for with the deepest anxiety by the other indicted regulators. Wilson is a Baptist preacher and a member of the Smyrna Church.

## Crowded with People

Ozark is full of people to-night, the camp-fires illuminating the commons surrounding the town. The Bald Knobbers attorneys attending court are Col. S.H. Boyd, O.H. Travers, F.M. Wolf, J.J. Gideon, and S.R. Bridges of Springfield, and D.M. Payne, of Ozark. The testimony on the motion for a change of venue, which will be filed as soon as the Knobber murder cases are called, will probably occupy the remainder of the week. Over 500 witnesses have now been summoned in the Knobber cases alone, and scarcely a voter will be left at home in the eastern section of the county.

## 12

# TRIAL OF GILBERT APPLEGATE

September 1, 1887.—Court convened at 1:30 o'clock this afternoon, with every seat in the room occupied, the crowd having taken possession of all the available space some time in advance of the Sheriff's announcement that Judge Hubbard was on the bench. The defendant, Gilbert Applegate, was ordered to be brought into court and all attorneys in the case called by the Sheriff.

The Court then took the panel of forty men and called the names of those elected to try the case. Much interest had been manifested by the crowd in the prospective jury, while the attorneys had been making their challenges, and each man

An 1887 newspaper illustration of Judge Walter D. Hubbard. *NewspaperArchive.com.*

was scrutinized closely as his name was called. When the jury had been polled, the following twelve men sat in the box to try the defendant, Gilbert Applegate, who now exhibited a decided interest in the legal drama about to open: H.G. Gilmore, John Lawson, J.H. Mills, William Mariey, Ansel Melton, Wm. Haislip, Thos. Hanks, Jas. Henry, J.H. Blevens, W.B. Mills, Tillman Wallace and Joshua Flood. The oldest man on the jury is about 50, and the youngest 28. All are married but two, and all are farmers except one, who is a miller. There is not a man from the eastern or southeastern sections of the county on the jury, and the majority of them live in Finley Township. It is a very fair jury with respect to intelligence and character, and some of its members are men of considerable prominence in the county.

## THE WITNESSES

At 2:15 p.m. the jury was sworn and then the State's witnesses were called in court. They were James Edens, Elizabeth Edens, George Green, Elizabeth Green, Amanda Green, Nancy J. Green, Wm. Johns, John Nash, Mat Nash, James R. McGuire, Andrew Hiles, Jack Hiles, W.J. Ray, Larkin Ray, Rev. T.A. Foster, Coroner J.P. Ralston, Dr. J.H. Fulbright, Morgan Bell, Hon. D.M. Cowan, J.C. Rogers, Judge Reuben, C.C. Clements, Archibald Mayden, Dr. E.B. Brown, James Preston, Wm. Abbott and T.L. Robertson. Jesse Robertson did not respond to his name, and the State ordered subpoenas for several additional witnesses. The witnesses were sworn, put under the rule and told to retire from the court-room.

The defense then called a long roll of witnesses, and the following persons filed up the aisle in front of his Honor: E.T. Abbott, Judge Hale, W.S. Smith, Samuel Turner, Jesse Mogart, John Mogart, William Abbott, John Nash, Mat Nash, J.L. Lee, Thomas Evans, J.S. Johnson, Nelson Stewart, Houston Simmons, J.F. Eddleman, Thomas Nix, George Dorland, Joseph Abbott, Richard St. John, J.J. Bruton and M.V. Abbott.

The defendants announced that they would use witness Joe Inman and Charley Graves, two of the men charged in the indictment. The Judge gave the Sheriff the most rigid orders about keeping order in the court-room, and told him to bring any one forward if seen talking and he would fine the offender. The rope was stretched across the room, just behind the bar, to keep the crowd back, but this had to be taken down to enable the witnesses to pass in and out.

## The Indictment Read

Everything being now ready the Court ordered the indictment read to the jury. Col. Almus Harrington, associate State counsel, in a very impressive manner read the document, which describes the tragedy of the night of the 11th of last March, charging the defendant, Gilbert Applegate, and fifteen members of the Chadwick Bald Knobber band with the murder of Charles Green. Col. Harrington then, in a brief statement to the jury, laid the foundation of the case the State proposed to establish.

He said the prosecution would prove that on the night of the 11th of March last, Dave Walker, William Walker, John Mathews, Wiley Mathews, C.O. Simmons, William Stanley, William Newton, Andy Adams, James Mathews and a number of others met at the old smelter on the head of Bull Creek, near Sparta, Christian County, Mo., and after holding a council masked themselves, and armed with shotguns and pistols, proceeded to the house of William Edens, one of the murdered men. Not finding William Edens at home, the band went at once to James Edens', father of the deceased. On reaching the home of James Edens the band made an attack on the house from the front and rear, shooting first through the window and breaking down both doors simultaneously, they rushed in, and by repeated shots killed William Edens and Charley Green.

An 1887 newspaper illustration of Colonel Almus "Babe" Harrington. *NewspaperArchive.com.*

Mr. Harrington said the State would also show in the assault on the family that James Edens was shot through the neck, scalped with his own ax, and left for dead. Here Mr. Bridges objected to Col. Harrington's description as to the manner in which James was wounded, reminding him that the word "scalped" did not appear in the indictment.

When Col. Harrington had finished, Senator S.R. Bridges arose for the defense, and said at the proper time they would make a statement of their case. He said, "All we ask of you now, gentlemen, is that you hold your minds free from prejudice till you hear the evidence."

## The First Witness

James Edens was then put on the witness stand and told the following story:

> I am 53 years old, and on the night of the 11th of last March lived three miles east of Sparta, in Christian County. There were present that night at my house myself and wife, my son William and his wife, my son-in-law Charles Green and his wife, besides my little grandchildren. My daughter-in-law, Amanda Green, had been sick for some time, and when we had been sitting up with her. At the time of the attack was made on my house there was dim light burning in the room. I was awakened by the noise of men near the house, and heard voices calling:
> "Get up ——— you, and come out, or we will kill every one of you."
> My son jumped out of bed immediately, and said: "Get up, pap, the Bald Knobbers are here."

*Left*: An 1887 newspaper illustration of Mr. James Edens. *NewspaperArchive.com*; *Right*: An 1887 newspaper illustration of Mrs. Elizabeth Edens. *NewspaperArchive.com*.

# Christian County

*In an instant the only window in the house was knocked in, and two or three shots fired through it. At the same time both doors were battered down and a band of ten or fifteen masked men rushed into the house, firing as they came. When the first shot was fired through the window I sprang for my pistol, which had already been taken by my wife. By this time three of the men had hold of me, trying to wretch the pistol from my hand. I jerked loose from all but one, who still held one of my arms. I then leveled my pistol on one of the men I had shoved away from me and attempted to fire.*

## Knocked Senseless

*At that instant a man struck me on the head with an ax, and some one shot me through the neck. I remember no more of what happened that night. It was as late as 8 o'clock next morning before I recovered consciousness. When I became conscience I saw my son, William Edens, and Charles Green lying on the floor of my house, dead. The floor was covered with blood.*

*I do not know whether I fired my pistol when I aimed it at one of the men, as the blow on the head just then knocked me senseless. I think even as many as ten men were in the house when I was struck and shot. All were masked.*

The witness here described the masks worn by the assailants, and the Sheriff was ordered to bring one of the regulating caps found hid near Chadwick after the fatal raid into the court-room.

The witness identified the mask as the same as worn by the band that killed his son and son-in-law. An ax was also shown to the witness, which, he said, was the one left in his house on the night of the killing.

Mr. Edens said this was his own ax and left on the floor of the house covered with blood and hair after the assault.

On cross-examination Mr. Edens said he had testified before the Coroner's Court the day after the killing, but it seemed all like a dream now. He knew there was no shooting from within the house till the men rushed in at the doors firing; did not know of any one of his family fired a shot; knew he was aiming to shoot when struck with the ax. His son William owned a pistol, but he did not know he had it with him that night. He could be mistaken about the window being broken and two or three shots fired through it before the doors were knocked down.

The defense gave Mr. Edens a very light cross-examination and the old man was not on the stand more than two hours.

## Mrs. Green's Testimony

An 1887 newspaper illustration of Mrs. Amanda Green. *NewspaperArchive.com.*

Mrs. Amanda M. Green, wife of Charles Green, deceased, was called next. She told the same story of the attack on the house that was given by Mr. Edens, but related many horrible details of the butchery which the old man could not witness.

She heard the shout of the hand: "Get up —— you, and come out or we will kill you!" Heard the window glass broken as though punched with something, when the firing began. Soon both doors were battered down and the band rushed into the house; soon some of the men had hold of her husband, when he fell; she caught one of the men and in the struggle with him pulled of his mask. Then the man aimed a gun at her breast and she pushed it aside as it fired. She was shot in the finger, and her clothes set afire by the blaze of the gun. She rubbed the fire out with her hands. Her husband was shot through the temple, and her brother through the head and body.

After the men left the house she found her husband and brother dead on the floor and old man Edens lying on the bed shot through the neck and wounded on the head with an ax.

For eight weeks previous to the killing the witness had been sick with the measles, and the Sunday before her husband had brought her to James Edens' in a wheelbarrow. She said after the killing a double-barreled shotgun was lying on the floor. It had been left by the men who made the attack on the house.

The witness was shown a gun which she identified as the one left in the house by its having one hammer broken and a piece fitted into the stock where the breech had been mended. The defense declined to cross-examine Mrs. Green.

## Emma Edens on the Stand

Mrs. Emma Edens, wife of William Edens, told the same story of the massacre, adding a fresh horror to the night's bloody history in describing the last act of the tragedy. She said one of the men fired at her and she fell back against the wall of the house, stunned by the discharge of the gun; when she got up she saw her husband lying near the fireplace, on his side. She went upon to his side, and he was alive. There was but one man in the house then, and he went out the door and some one said, "Put it to him again." A man poked a gun in at the door and shot him through the head. After this last shot her husband drew only three breaths.

She saw Amanda Green's clothes on fire, and heard old Mrs. Edens say, "Amanda, you are burning up."

Then Amanda put out the fire by rubbing her clothes with her hands.

*Left*: An 1887 newspaper illustration of William "Will" Edens. *NewspaperArchive.com*; *Right*: An 1887 newspaper illustration of Mrs. Emma Edens, widow. *NewspaperArchive.com*.

## George Green Examined

An 1887 newspaper illustration of Mr. George W. Green. *NewspaperArchive.com.*

George Green said he lived a quarter of a mile from James Edens, and heard the shooting on the night of the 11th of March; heard two shots—first very distinctly; called his wife and said, "Mother, get up; the Bald knobbers are on."

He thought at first the firing was not at Edens'; then heard several other shots, less distinctly, as they seemed to be in the house; the shots sounded dull; heard the screaming of two women, and started to Edens' at once; met the masked men on their way leaving Edens' house; some were riding, others on foot. As he passed them, one man halted and said: "Where are you going?" Told them he was not going far. One man said: "Then Will Green had better go d——n quick."

Arriving at the house he found William Edens and Charley Green lying on the floor dead and old man Edens on the bed senseless. He then went for one of the neighbors and had a doctor sent for. Saw the gun on the floor and found blood in several places outside the house.

## A Mother's Story

An 1887 newspaper illustration of Mrs. Mary J. Green. *NewspaperArchive.com.*

Mrs. Mary J. Green, wife of George Green, and mother of the deceased, told the same story about what she saw at the house when she got there. She identified the gun in Edens' house on the night of the killing.

Arch Mayden, Mrs. Nancy Bridges, Andrew Lasley, a member of the Coroner's jury that held the inquest, and Dr. J.P. Ralston, Coroner of Christian County, described the manner in which Edens and Green were shot.

Mr. Mayden explained why he did not go to Edens' house immediately on hearing the noise, by saying he was afraid. He heard of the killing about 12 o'clock, but did not go to the house till near 3. He lived a short distance from the scene of the killing.

The witnesses being disposed of much faster than expected, the State may close to-morrow. Applegate is attended by his wife and baby. The wife and sister of C.O. Simmons sit by the side of Mrs. Applegate.

## 13

# APPLEGATE ACQUITTED

Sept. 6, 1887.—The argument in the Applegate cases began last night at 8 o'clock, Col. Harrington opened for the state. T.J. Delaney followed for the defense. The court-room was densely crowed, all of the survivors of the Edens-Green family occupied front seats immediately behind the bar. Old Mrs. Edens, the mother of William Edens, and the widows of the two murdered men, were deeply affected by the State's recital of the horrid butchery. The women wept constantly while the tragedy was being detailed by the prosecution counsel, and the bereaved mother, whose memory of the bloody scene was refreshed by the speaker's summing up of the evidence in the case, almost swooned from agony. James Edens and George Green, the fathers of the two slain men, gazed on the speakers with stern, tearless eyes, and seemed to feast with eager relish on the words of vengeance that fell from the lips of the State's advocates.

Applegate was attended by his wife and eight children. The defendant did not blanch under the fierce denunciation of his legal accusers, and listened without the tremor of a nerve to the arguments connecting him with the murder.

Court convened at 8 o'clock this morning and argument for the State was resumed by J.J. Brown, Hon. J.J. Gideon and D.M. Payne followed for the defense and J.A. Hammond for the State. In the afternoon Hon. S.R. Bridges, senior counsel for the defense, and Prosecuting Attorney, and at 4:10 p.m. the case was given to the jury.

At 5:30 the twelve men who had retired to the jury-room over the jail were seen filing down the stairway, and then there was a general rush to the

Court House, each man among the crowd around the public square eager to secure a seat so that he could hear the verdict. The jury passed into the courtroom and took the seats they had occupied for five days, and the Sheriff was ordered to bring Applegate again before his peers. The twenty-three Bald Knobber prisoners in jail were pale with excitement, and as many of them as had the freedom of the outside corridor crowded around the grated windows fronting the Court House and looked anxiously after Applegate as the Sherriff conducted him to the bar of justice. The prisoner still wore that stolid air that has marked his demeanor with a deliberate and steady step. When the jury had been polled the oldest man of the number handed Judge Hubbard the verdict, which the clerk read as follows:

> *We, the jury, find the defendant not guilty in manner as charged in the indictment.*
> *(signed)*
>
> JOSHUA FLOOD.
> FORMAN. [*sic*]

Applegate rose up to receive the congratulations of his attorney, and now showed more excitement than any time during the trial. He was taken back to jail, as the indictment of murder of William Edens still stands against him, and on the Court House steps the prisoner's wife and children came up with the happy husband and father. His fellow prisoners greeted him with the warmest congratulations as he entered the corridor.

The verdict was not a surprise to many, as the instructions of the Court excluded the findings of any lower degree of crime than that charged in the indictment.

There is no dissatisfaction expressed on account of the verdict, as everybody is now convinced that the real murderers of Charles Green and W. Edens will, in due time, be punished according to their desserts. The trial of Gilbert Applegate has laid bare the secrets of that revolting crime, and the men who planned and executed the assault on the Eden-Green family are now in the Ozark Jail.

This ends for the present the Bald Knobber trials, as there is not time to take another case, though the Davis boys are anxious to have a hearing. Court will probably adjourn to-morrow. Applegate will be released on bail, and the other cases against him may be nolle pros'd at the next term of court.

## 14

# QUINTUPLE LYNCHING

Nov. 15, 1888.—A special—from Ozark, Christian county, this state, gives the following details of the quintuple lynching, last night, by Bald Knobbers of witnesses against Dave Walker and other leaders of that organization. Ames Wilson, a farmer living near Chadwick, on the Ozark range, came into Ozark this morning after five coffins, which were to be used to bury the victims of the vengeance of the Bald Knobbers. Far from the nearest town, in the shadow of the Ozark range, lived the men who had been instrumental in bringing justice to the murderous leaders of the organization, and since the trials, which resulted in the apparent demoralization of the band, these men have lived in the belief that their troubles were over.

This morning sun, however, shone on a sight that proved conclusively that the law defying organization still existed. From the limbs of a mighty oak tree on the banks of a creek, only a short distance from the place of the Green and Eden murder,

### FIVE CORPSES WERE SWINGING

in the breeze, and each one bore the dread symbol of death at the hands of the Bald Knobber, a knife-cut across the brow. A farmer who was early on his way to town was the first to see the horrible sight, and he quickly summoned his neighbors, who took down the bodies and found them to be those of

Charles Green, James Eden, William Enders, Jonathan Wiley and Emmett Anderson. All these men had sworn to the facts of the killing of Green and Eden, brothers of the first named, and on their evidence Dave Walker was sentenced to pay the extreme penalty of the law. The bodies were placed in a wagon and carried to the homes of their families, and there the story of the latest Bald Knobber raid was heard. At the home of Green and Eden, who occupied jointly a long, double log house, all was terror and dismay. As soon as the wails of the bereaved women and children could be stilled, the following was told to the horrified listeners. At precisely 12 o'clock a knock was heard at the door, and in response to an inquiry the family [was] told that a neighbor had a stalled wagon near by, and requested assistance. Green and Eden immediately went out, and as they passed the gate, a single

## PISTOL SHOT WAS HEARD

and out into the moonlight, from the bushes rode about 200 Bald Knobbers with the disguise that a year ago was so well known in the Southwest. They surrounded the two unfortunate men, a slight struggle followed, and then all rode away with their victims. The terrorized family could do nothing and were afraid to stir out of doors until daylight. At the residence of Enders much the same story was told. At Wiley's house the demand for admittance was refused and the Bald Knobbers broke down the door and dragged the man from the house. During the melee several shots were fired at the assailing party by the members of the family, and they are confident that one of the raiders was wounded. Anderson was captured while on his way home from Chadwick. The whole country is again under a reign of terror, as no one knows who did the deed, and each is distrustful of his neighbor. Sheriff Williams has gone to the scene of the murders with a large posse of men, and says he will hunt down the perpetrators of the deed if it is possible. The only clue is the Bald Knobber, who is supposed to be wounded.

## 15

# HOW THE MATTER STANDS

### December 18th, 1888

After long trials and much labor on the part of the State, the following results have been achieved:

David Walker was convicted of murder and sentenced to death. An appeal to the Supreme Court was taken. His case has not been acted on.

William Walker was likewise convicted and sentenced. The Supreme Court has reviewed the appeal taken and has confirmed the sentence, and Sat., Dec. 28 as the day of his execution. He will, perhaps, be reprieved, so that all may hang on the same day.

Wiley Mathews was in like manner convicted and sentenced. His appeal is now before the Supreme Court.

John Mathews was convicted and sentenced to death. His case has been reviewed, the sentence confirmed, and Jan. 11 next set as the day of his execution.

The Rev. C.O. Simmons pleaded guilty of murder in the second degree. On account of previous good character he was let off with twelve years in the State prison.

William Stanley and Amos Jones entered a like plea and were sent to prison for twenty-one years. All of the rest of those indicted are out on bonds, save Lewis Davis, who is wholly free on a nolle, and Gilbert Applegate, who was tried and acquitted because he was a long way from the house when the firing began, and tried to get Chief Dave Walker to stop it. Those out on bonds, the people say, will never be tried. They all testified for the State.

If the condemned men hang, and their attorney here says he has very little hope for them, although still at work, it is feared that the Knobbers will shoot the witnesses and prosecuting officers as fast as convenient. If they don't hang, the Taney county Knobbers, whose numbers are great enough to enable them to control the county, will, it is said, complete the work they had on hand when the death of Kinney and the prosecution of the Christian county murderers made it advisable to stop. That work is to rid the county of all its "objectionable" inhabitants.

## THE BALD KNOBBER TERRITORY

The operations of the Bald Knobbers spread over the counties of Taney, Ozark, Stone, Douglas, and Christian, and it is assorted that one company existed in Greene county, with members even in the city of Springfield. It is the Thirteenth Senatorial district of the State. It is certain that one man named Graham was killed in Greene county, but the people there deny that it was a Bald Knob murder, and there is nothing but Taney county rumor to place against this denial.

The territory involved is eighty-five miles long, along the Arkansas line, and spreads back just forty miles to the northern borders of Christian and Douglas counties. A glance at any good map of Missouri will show that, except for a little spur running-down from Springfield as far as Chadwick, Christian county, the region is without railroads, and as for this spur, it has but one train a day, and that is scheduled for three hours to cover its length of thirty-five miles, but it more frequently takes four.

In Christian county the Ozark Mountains are about like the Orange Mountains of New Jersey for height. The land is fertile, and produces all sorts of grain and fruits with very little labor. Douglas county is much the same and both are filling up with settlers.

Taney and the other border counties are mountainous, but are fertile in the bottoms along the streams. The low hills are covered with scrub and post oaks; the mountain peaks are bald knobs that gleam in the sun. The hills are supposed to be as well filled with lead as the cemeteries are known to be. The principal crops are corn and cotton. All kinds of fruits thrive.

## The Dead—Taney County

J. M. Everett, Forsyth, shot to death by Al Layton.
Amus Ring, shot to death by Newton Herrell.
Frank Taylor, hanged by the Bald Knobbers.
Tubal Taylor, hanged by the Bald Knobbers.
Mack Dimmock, shot to death by William Taylor for a horse and Buggy worth $60.
Buck Mercer, shot to death by Deputy Sherriff Arthur Kissee, who was endeavoring to arrest him.
Andrew Coggburn, shot to death by Capt. N.N. Kinney, the chief of the Bald Knobbers.
Sam Snapp, shot to death by Wash Middleton.
James Manus, a Deputy Sherriff, shot to death by James Brooks, whom he was trying to arrest.
James Brown, shot to death by James Bench.
Wash Middleton, shot to death by Deputy Sheriff James L. Holt.
George Warren, stabbed to death by Claude Layton.
Capt. Kinney, shot to death by William Miles Jr.

## The Wounded—Taney County

John T. Dickinson, shot through the mouth and neck and right shoulder by Frank Taylor.
Mrs. John T. Dickinson, end of first finger of right hand shot off by Frank Taylor.
Reuben Pruitt, shot through the body by Deputy Sherriff George Taylor.

## The Killed—Christian County

Charles Green, shot to death by the Bald Knobbers.
William Edens, shot to death by the Bald Knobbers.
Bob Patterson, hit over the head with a revolver, and skull fractured by the Bald Knobbers during a whipping.

## The Wounded – Christian County

James Edens, shot in the neck and cut scars on the top of the head by the Bald Knobbers.

Mrs. Melvina Green, end of right forefinger shot off by the bald Knobbers.

## "Just Quiet Between Shots"

A reporter was about to leave Taney's county seat [and] said, "Well, neighbor, everything seems to be all quiet here now."

A citizen pronouncing the syllables with his lips closed: "Um-hum-m-m. Um-hum-m-m it is quite-like as damn quite, stranger; jest quiet between shots."

## 16
# SET FREE BY FRIENDS

Dec. 20, 1888.—Bald Knobbers broke open the jail last night and released John and Wiley Mathews, who were there under sentence of death, and five other prisoners. The four Bald Knobbers who were sentenced to hang for the murder of Charles Green and William Edens on March 11, 1887, were David Walker, better known in Christian county as "Bull Creek Dave," William Walker, his son, John Mathews and Wiley Mathews, his nephews. None of the condemned [has] reached [his] fiftieth year, and Wm. Walker is not yet nineteen years of age. The condemned were to have been executed on May 18, 1888, but on an appeal to the supreme court they escaped the gallows temporarily. Last October the supreme court affirmed the decision of the Christian county circuit court and fixed Dec. 28 as the day of execution. The sensational trial turned attention to the Bald-Knobbers from all quarters, and the history of the organization was made public. Taney county, Missouri, is noted as the Birthplace of Baldknobberism.

### UTTER DEMORALIZATION ENSUED

After due warning from the Bald-Knobbers, which was disregarded, one bright night in the summer of 1886, the famous regulators entered Chadwick's house and emptied the liquors belonging to the saloon into the streets. Later on this was repeated and the traffic broken up. There were numerous visits by the band to petty offenders, but nothing occurred to attract widespread attention until the Green-Eden affair, which terminated in the downfall of Bald-Knobbism. The Green-Edens killing occurred in March, 1887. At a point eight miles southeast of Ozark, near the Edens' dwelling, John Evans was whipped by the Bald Knobbers for misbehaving in church. Old man Eden, a friend of Evans, interfered and received four blows with the whip before Chief Walker interfered. This so enraged Edens that he fearlessly condemned the Bald-Knobbers, and on the night of March 10, 1887, the band met to consider Edens' offenses. There were twenty-six present, and, after brief deliberation, they proceeded to the Edens residence to punish the inmates. They were met by resistance, and fired several volleys into the house, killing William Edens and Charles Green, his brother-in-law, and seriously wounding old man Edens. In the melee young Walker was shot in the leg. The outrage brought about a culmination of public indignation, and Zach Johnson, the fearless sheriff of Christian county, with a picked posse, started after the murderers, and, within forty-eight hours, had all save Bill Walker under arrest. He was, captured three weeks later in Douglas county, where he had gone for safety. At that time there was

## No Jail in Ozark

and the prisoners were taken to Springfield, Mo., for safekeeping. A jail was promptly built, however, and the Bald Knobbers transferred to Ozark, from which place two of their number escaped last night. The first hearing of the Bald Knobber cases was in August, 1887, but Chief Walker was not tried until April, 1888. In March, 1887, three of the prisoners confessed, so the trial of Dave Walker was merely formal, he admitting the assault of the Bald Knobbers on the Eden home, but pleading he did not arrive until after the shooting had ceased. One of the most peculiar features of Bald Knobbism is that the majority of the prominent members of the band are devout church members. Especially is this true of Chief Walker, who was a temperance advocate and a generally devout man. He can not see yet that the Bald Knob regulators were other than champions of the right, who made a fatal but unavoidable mistake in the Green-Eden killing. He has asserted confidently all along that he would never be hanged.

## 17

# PRISONERS AT LARGE & STARVED

Dec. 30, 1888.—The fugitive Knobbers who escaped from the jail yesterday morning are still at large in spite of the most vigilant efforts of Sheriff Johnson and posse for their capture. The vicinity of the Mathews' home was diligently searched yesterday and guards placed at the passes to the hills in which it was believed the men would try to find shelter. Some boys hunting rabbits two miles from Ozark yesterday came upon a man lying low in a fallen tree top. He seemed very pale and excited, but explained to the boys that he had hidden to scare them and have some fun. After telling them that his name was Bill Owens he went off into the woods and the boys told the story; and a posse of men vainly hunted the woods in the vicinity. From the boys' description the hidden man was John Mathews. At 1 o'clock this morning a man calling himself Owens called at the house of James Collins, four miles south of Ozark, and said he was hunting work. Collins kept the man till morning and gave him his breakfast. Observing that his strange guest carried two pistols, Collins soon came to the conclusion that the man was one of the escaped Knobbers, and came to Ozark and notified Sheriff Johnson, who at once went with a party of armed men to that vicinity. It is believed that this man will surely be caught before morning. The work at the jail is believed to have been planned by Bill Newton, who was at one time a turnkey at the jail, and could have easily taken an impression of the key.

## Captured & Nearly Starved

Jan. 1, 1889.—John Mathews one of the condemned Bald Knobbers was released from the jail here a few nights ago was brought back yesterday by James Collins who captured him on the road three miles south of Ozark on Sunday night. He was almost exhausted by hunger and cold having had but one meal since he left the jail and had become dazed lost and was all broke up. He knows about his nephew, Wiley Mathews, but from other sources it has been learned that he, in company with number of other friends were seen on Sunday twenty miles from here on their way to Taney county. It is not expected that he will be retaken very soon as he is a resolute, determined man, and is evidently among friends who will shield him from the officers and help him to resist any attempts to capture him. Sheriff Johnson and his deputies have returned to town, and, perhaps [will] go out again for some days. A guard will be placed around the jail from now until [the] time Bald Knobbers are finally disposed of.

John Mathews says he does not know who released him and his companions from the jail. All scattered in different directions when they got out. William Bedford, one of the railroad car robbers who left the jail with the Mathews[es], voluntarily returned last evening saying it was better to be in jail than to starve and freeze outside. He was locked up.

## 18

# BUNGLING WORK OF AN EXECUTION

May 10, 1889.—The three Bald Knobbers, Dave Walker, better known in Christian county as "Bull Creek Dave," chief of the Bald Knobbers, his son William Walker, and John Mathews, were hanged for the murder of Charles Green and William Edens, March 11, 1887.

They were firmly of the opinion, up to within forty-eight hours of the execution, that they would never be called upon to pay the extreme penalty of a life for a life. None of the trio had yet reached his fiftieth year, and William Walker was barely 19 years of age. The three men, together with Wiley Mathews, nephew of John, were to have been hanged on May 18, 1888, but on an appeal to the supreme court they were given a temporary escape from the gallows. Last October the supreme court affirmed the decision of [the] Christian county circuit court, and fixed December 28 an account of which appeared in these dispatches.

About April 12, the attorneys for Bill Walker and John Mathews made a strong appeal for the commutation of the sentence of their clients, and when that was denied, asked for a respite to May 10, the date of Dave Walker's execution, which was granted. For the past two weeks powerful pleas have been made to Governor Francis for the commutation of the sentences of the three men. On Wednesday last, after reviewing the case at length, the governor declined to interfere further, and the condemned men were notified that they must die.

Dave Walker and his son Bill received the news calmly and with the nerve that has always sustained them, but Mathews broke down completely, and wept like a child.

The three Bald Knobbers, were executed at the jail in Ozark. The execution was an awful butchery, the ropes stretching—breaking and all, having to be carried to the scaffold again.

The jury and reporters were admitted to the inside at 9:20 o'clock. Just before leaving his cell John Mathews proclaimed his innocence in a loud voice. The sheriff helped Mathews up the steps, young Walker followed with a firm step, his father following close behind as firm as ever.

## Final Preparations

The carpenters gave the scaffold its finishing touches last evening and everything was ready by 8 o'clock. William Walker, one of the condemned Bald Knobbers, was baptized at 6 p.m., by immersion in a bath basin carried into the jail. The scene was very affecting. John Mathews made a long prayer which could be distinctly heard in the streets fronting the jail.

The prisoners ate their supper with as much relish as usual and appeared very well, except Mathews, who took his fate very hard. He passed a restless night praying at short intervals, asking the Lord to give him strength to go through the ordeal and claiming that he was a martyr. He did not sleep over two hours during the night.

Hangman's noose. *Creative Commons, Stephen J. Conn.*

The two Walkers retired about 11 o'clock, went to sleep and did not wake until after 4 o'clock. They stated that they rested well. They were up early and ate their breakfast at the usual hour. The jail yard was full of guards armed with Winchesters, shotguns and revolvers and were in the charge of Captain G.W. Taylor, who was foreman of the grand jury which indicted the Bald Knobbers.

Mathews' wife and mother came in last evening and several others of his friends are here.

Divine services were opened in the jail at 7:30 o'clock. They were conducted by Rev. S. Thomas Hands, D.E. Graystone and T.B. Howe, assisted by a few Christian ladies. Mathews took part in the exercise and delivered an earnest prayer in a loud voice. William Walker also led in prayer.

At 8:53 o'clock the sheriff entered the jail and read the death warrants to the doomed men, after which Thomas Denny, one of their attorneys, was admitted to have an interview and bid them farewell. John Mathews came to the window and had a conversation with a correspondent. He said:

> *I have to die, but thank God I can say I am innocent and have told the truth all along about this matter. I have nothing to regret. I went out through the hole not because I was guilty but to escape a shameful death, but it was the will of God that I should die and I ought to be proud of it. I was a soldier in the federal army and I am proud of my record. I am willing for the people who have known me all my life to say what kind of a man I have been.*

At 9:19 o'clock the prisoners commenced dressing themselves for the scaffold. They were dressed with white shirts, linen collars, black cravats, low slippers, and black coats, vests and pants.

## Just Before The Drop

At the drop a short prayer was delivered by Rev. T.B. Horn, after which all joined in singing. Rev. T.B. Horn rendered a selection from the book of Job. Rev. Thomas Hanks delivered a beautiful prayer.

The noose was adjusted at 9:40. John Mathews said he had nothing to add; he was there but took no part in the crime. Mathews called on all who were willing to help his little ones to hold up their hands. Nearly every one in his sight held up their hands. The black caps were adjusted at 9:51, and at 9:53 the drop fell.

## Absolute Butchery!

John Mathews fell praying. The stretch of the rope let all fall to the ground; the rope broke and William Walker fell loose and lay there, struggling and groaning. He talked for three minutes, when he was taken up by the sheriff and deputies on the scaffold.

Dave Walker was drawn up and died in about fifteen minutes. Mathews lived about thirteen minutes and died, with his feet on the ground. The scene was horrible in the extreme.

Mathews and Dave Walker were cut down at 10:10. The rope was again adjusted and William Walker lifted helpless and groaning and gurgling, almost insensible, the rope again adjusted and the trap again sprung. This time he came to a sudden stop with his feet full three inches from the ground, and he died without a struggle.

An 1889 newspaper title, "Bungling Work." *Library of Congress.*

## Records and Pedigrees

"Bull Creek" Dave Walker, according to his own story, was born in Christian county, Kentucky, in June, 1843. His parents moved to Christian county, Missouri, when he was four years old and settled near Sparta. The section they settled on was at that time a part of Greene county. They had a hard life, up to the war. Dave enlisted in Company M, Sixth Missouri Volunteers, in 1862, but, after a few months' service, was discharged, as he was under age. He went back home, but had a stronger inclination for war than ever, and enlisted in Company H, of the Sixteenth Missouri. His age was not found out and he went through the war. After the war he returned to Bull Creek and entered forty acres of government land. This was his homestead. He joined the Bald Knobbers three years ago, when the first company was formed in Christian county (then Bull Creek county), and was made the chief. He claimed that beside[s] the pouring out of liquor at the Chadwick saloon and the whipping of John Evans for "cutting up in church," his company had not done any regulating. It was the whipping of Evans which excited the hostility of the Edens.

William Walker is the oldest son of the Bald Knobber. He was born in March, 1870. He lived on the farm with his father all his life, and joined the Bald Knobbers at the same time. He was wounded in the right groin in the Green-Edens killing, and that night was taken to his uncle's house, in Douglass county. He was captured later by Sheriff Johnson, with the assistance of J.D. Newton, a brother of Walker's sweetheart.

John Mathews was born on Bull creek, in Christian county, Mo., five miles from Chadwick, April 19, 1843. He was in the Union army during the war, enlisted in the Forty-sixth Missouri. He took part in several engagements in occurrence to Gen. Price's raid. He had nine children, most of them are small. He was a member of the Baptist church, and had been a Bald Knobber but two months when the shooting occurred. His son Jimmie, fourteen years old, was at the Edens house the night of the killing, and was indicted with his father, but was released by the court after furnishing a bond of $1,000 on account of his youth.

## 19

## A KNOBBER MELODRAMA

An interesting circumstance growing out of the Knobber organization is the writing and printing of a melodrama by a number of citizens of Sparta. Twelve men were engaged in producing this work, five of whom were Bald Knobbers. It was simply an effort to realize cold cash out of the misdeeds of themselves and their associates. When the play was written a stock company with a paid-up capital of $500 was organized. The company was composed of the authors. They intended to act the different parts themselves, and to spend the whole of that $500, if necessary, in going to New York, hiring a theater, painting suitable scenery, buying posters and space in the papers, and stirring up the city generally.

But the play was a partial exposé of the secrets of the order, and the fact that it had been written got bruited about, and raised such a storm among the other Knobbers that the project of taking New York by storm and $500 had to be abandoned until the matter cooled. More than that it is said to be all that a man's life is worth here to show a copy of the pamphlet to a man not a Knobber.

A reporter read it through. It was to have been realistic to the most minute detail. Thus in act 3, scene 1, where the Taylor boys were to be lynched, two men were to be actually strung from a limb of tree. Knobber vanity was to be gratified by using the names of the author-actors in the play. The pamphlet has twenty-five pages of forty-five lines each, and an average of ten words to the line. It is proposed to rewrite the pamphlet—so as to lighten up its blood-and-thunder darkness by inserting a part for a comedian.

## 20

# KNOBBERS & THE ANTI

## Waging War

March 3, 1890.—Taney county was the seat of the Bald Knobber war and as the state has effectually quelled that trouble by the execution of the leaders of the murderous raids the people have adopted one of the favorite pastimes of their neighbors across the Western state line.

Preparations are now being made for what will probably be a hotly contested county seat fight which with the well known inclination of the South Missourian will probably terminate disastrously for several of the participants. At the last session of the state legislature an act was passed granting the sum of $5,000 for the purpose of building a courthouse in Taney county. This is a big lot of money for that county and at once there arose a scramble from the various parts of the county to see which section would have the pleasure of handling it and possibly retaining the "sweat" on their hands from the use of it.

Taney City a little town about five miles from Forsythe, the present county seat, became the strongest aspirant for the honors and at last the fight became narrowed down to these two cities. Numerously signed petitions were sent into the county clerk praying for an election to decide the question but the county court concluded that if there was anything done it would be by themselves and the result was that the whole year has been wasted in getting ready to decide the matter by the full bench. The greater the delay the more difficult became the decision, for the judges saw that they had a blight on their hands whichever way they voted. The old jealousies broke out afresh and there was a certainty of a bloody fight as soon as the decision was made. About two weeks ago the matter was brought to a termination and an immense crowd gathered at Forsythe for the purpose of hearing the decision of the judges. But here came another disappointment. The judge from the eastern part of the county was absent. He sent word that sickness would prevent his attendance. As the two remaining judges were divided on the "Question," one being from Forsythe and the other from Taney City, the vote of the third judge was necessary to locate the county seat.

Court was adjourned for three days but when that time expired the judge was still absent and a courier was sent to inquire after his health. It was then discovered that sickness of the mind was all that ailed him. He knew that on his decision rested the whole case as his ballot would break the tie. He had studied the matter over and came to the conclusion that his life was of more consequence to him than the county seat to the people and therefore he would stay at home and let them fight it out as best pleased the contending parties. Those who remember the circumstances of the last two years in Southern Missouri know that in Taney county there are two nonpolitical parties which have been in opposition for years. These are the Bald Knobbers and anti–Bald Knobbers. These two parties have taken up the fight and are at war over the location. This being the case, it can be readily seen why the judge was at a loss to know how to please both parties. On the last day that was set for the convening of the county court, the town was full of men representing both factions and when it was learned that the judge would not brave the people and cast his vote for either place, the members of both sides began filling themselves up on the white whisky which is only to be found in this section. The result was that the town was soon full of men who were fighting drunk.

A dozen or so ordinary fights on the streets occurred but it remained for the coming of night to bring a culmination of the trouble. One of the doggeries which by courtesy is called a "grocery" was full of a rough, pushing, swearing crowd of men who were excited over the question of spending that $5,000. Suddenly a blow was struck and instantly the room was converted into a bedlam. The lights were put out, and in the darkness the biting and gouging that went on was fearful. By mutual consent pistols seemed to be tabooed, but knives and teeth were brought into play with terrible effect. When the struggle died out from sheer exhaustion on the part of the combatants and the lights were brought in the scene that presented itself was horrible.

Blood covered everything. Men in all stages of stupor lay around the floor. Faces in all stages of mutilation were seen and the whole place had the appearance of a slaughter house. No one was killed but the wounds were of such serious nature that it will be many weeks before the participants of the free fight will fully recover from the effects of their debauch. But the county seat question is still undecided.

Taney county has a population of 5,000 and its indebtedness is $18,000. As the proportion of taxpayers to the population is small, this leaves the county in a very bad condition financially. County warrants are held at 40 cents on the dollar and hard to sell at any price. As there are eight men held for murder in the first degree and seven for second degree all of which cases are to be tried at the coming session of the circuit court, it is estimated that the county warrants will soon be worse than valueless to the holders.

*21*

# THE BALD KNOBBERS REIGN

May, 1891.—This little station, the present terminus of the White River branch of the St. Louis and San Francisco Railroad, is now lapsing into that obscurity from which the deeds of the Bald Knobbers brought the eastern section of Christian County into such prominence. The train from Springfield, Mo., makes its daily trip to the turntable here, stopping just long enough to hitch on a car or two loaded with wood or ties, the timber trade being the only traffic of any importance carried on at this point. Situated at the southern terminus of a narrow platen, or "divide," separating the two beautiful mountain rivulets Swan and Bull, Chadwick is a frontier station of the great world of commerce. It was here that the rugged aspect of nature disputed the further advance of railroad enterprise, and the adventurous little branch of the great Frisco line, after making its tortuous way thirty-five miles south of Springfield, paused on the summit of the table land overlooking the deep gorge through which flows Swan, one of the numerous crystal rivulets of White River. Five years ago, when the steam-whistle of the locomotive startled the deer and wolf of the hills, the dense forests of oak and pine surrounding the present site of Chadwick were almost untouched by the pioneer's axe. But with the railroad came the trade in timber and ties, and the farmers of Swan and Bull began to depend more on the axe and less on the dog and gun as a means of living.

It was here, among these tie and wood cutters, that the Bald Knobber organization was first formed in Christian County. It had already existed in Taney County for more than a year, and the fame of Capt. Nat. N.

Kinney, the Knobber chief of the White River Valley, had already spread over the country. He was a new and dauntless champion of the regulating idea in government. The first speech in Christian County in favor of the movement was made here by the White River leader, on a dry-goods box in front of the Chadwick Hotel, while his new regulating recruits stacked their guns around the rude rostrum and stood by to applaud every bold utterance in justification of the conduct of the night raiders. After this public demonstration in support of the Knobber policy the black-masque following increased rapidly around Chadwick, and in a few weeks the stronghold of the outlaw movement in Christian County was here.

So great was the demand for the hideous horned headgear worn by the Knobbers at their nightly gatherings that Dave Walker, the new recruiting chief of Christian County, could not supply his numerous followers around Chadwick until several women had been taken into the secret and their defter hands employed. During the summer of 1886 the craze was at its height. Everybody either had joined the secret order or maintained a discreet silence with regard to its frequent acts of violence.

Ministers of the gospel became the most enthusiastic members of the organization. They fancied they saw in the summary treatment of certain offenders a new and effective aid to the pulpit in the work of taming the unregenerate sons of this mountain fastness. The Knobber offered the most practical solution of the whisky question that had ever been presented to the Prohibitionists of the Ozark region. They solved it by marching in an armed masked body to the offending saloons and drawing the spigots and breaking the bottles. This was done twice to Chadwick by Chief Walker and his Knobber followers, and after the second raid nothing stronger than vinegar could be found here till the final collapse of the regulating movement.

Never were people more thoroughly deluded by a lawless infatuation than the simple people of this wild country who joined the organization. They really believed that a better system of government had been established and that the crude code of the regulating council was superior to the mandates of the legally constituted courts of law. The civil law was intricate and full of technicalities. Its processes were slow. Justice was often cheated. The heaviest pocket-book too often won. The new code was simpler, quicker and surer. It was to supplant the civil law. "We must not go to law with one another," was a fundamental proposition set forth by the Knobbers' government. They said [it] was too costly for the advantages it secured to the common citizen. Each community could regulate its own affairs without the expensive machinery of salaried courts and executive officers. The very crimes that most annoyed the poor, honest man the civil law did not suppress.

Hog stealing and whiskey selling had never been materially checked by the regular courts, and the thieving vagrant who depended on his nocturnal visits to a smoke-house and corn-crib for a living did not fear the county jail. The regulating hickory periodically applied to the bare back of such offenders was warranted a hundred prosecutions. And the petty thief and the prowling vagabond might thus be reached and reformed without burdening the already oppressed taxpayers.

Such was the simple philosophy of the deluded during the early days of the regulating movement before the inevitable tendency of the order to criminal violence and retaliatory vengeance became manifest to the better members of the oath-bound fraternity. Well-meaning men had sworn allegiance to the new regulating code, expecting that moderation and justice would rule the nightly councils of the black-mask order and give to each victim of the lash or rope "a fair trial" before the findings of the summary tribunal were executed. This was one of the boasted principles of the Knobber policy. Personal spite was to be rigidly excluded from all these inquisitorial proceedings and the scales of justice held dispassionately by the new guardian of the social order. Such was the solemn oath taken by the initiate as he stood at the threshold of the mystic order. No private enmity must influence his conduct as a Bald-Knobber in the administration of that simple justice which the courts of law had so signally failed to dispense among the people.

No wonder the unsophisticated mountaineers were beguiled by this artful promise of a new government in which money would not defeat the poor man's good cause and crime find an escape from a swift and sure punishment. Isolated from the great world of commerce and modern thought, by the influences of the daily newspaper and the telegraph, living in conformity with the traditions of an illiterate ancestry, with little or no education, these simple people were easily persuaded to join the ranks which bold men commanded. Their work at first was good. The order in a rude way enforced morality in the community. The trials under the *Regulating Code* were fair, and personal enmity entered little into the judgments. But the resentment, jealousies and spites of each actuated all; they fast sank from law enforcers in some sense to law breakers in every sense. A small cabal of desperadoes whom some faithful Knobbers still obeyed terrorized at pleasure and murdered at will. From such despotism amid anarchy, the community was sure to rid itself in time, or be killed in the attempt. Fortunately the Eden-Green massacre, pitiless and cold-blooded, aroused the law, long dethroned. Dave Walker and twenty-eight of his band were captured, and the reign of the Bald Knobbers was over.

Many rumors have been circulated about the reorganization of the black-mask order.

Those who are glad the Knobbers' reign is over are too many, and too many members of the organization are too glad they were not involved in the consequences of that murderous raid to take any new risk in the interest of their unfortunate clans, men who are now confined under sentence of death.

The Taney County champion of regulating, whose presence in Chadwick eighteen months ago would have created a greater sensation than a visit from President Cleveland, is regarded here with loathing. The poor women of Bull Creek, whose husbands, brothers and fathers have been taken from their homes to jail, regard Capt. Kinney and a few Baptist preachers of this county as the real cause of all their sorrow. Two wives from here, and near the head of Bull Creek, live the wife and daughter of the condemned Knobber chief, Dave Walker, earning their daily bread by doing the hardest outdoor work. The axe and the plough have become familiar to the hands of these poor women since the husband and son, father and brother, were arrested for the Eden-Green murder. Poverty and distress are in every cabin home where his faithful followers dwelt. Sorrow and ruin mark everywhere the downfall of the Knobber movement.

## 22

# MURDER OF MRS. JOHN WESLEY BRIGHT

March 31, 1892.—The murder of Mrs. John Wesley Bright and the lynching that followed illustrates the curious mental conditions that prevail here in the heart of the country where the Bald Knobbers originated and so many murders were committed in consequence. It is not likely that the lynchers were animated by the hates growing out of the fights that the Bald Knobbers were responsible for.

John Wesley Bright was a ranchman living on Roark Creek, a tributary of White River, in the western part of Taney county. He did not live on good terms with his wife, the trouble growing. It is alleged out of his liking for another woman. To end that trouble and clear the way for a marriage with another woman, Bright determined to kill his wife. He could do that with comparative safety from observation, because his place was isolated. That he was not deterred by the fear of punishment may be inferred from the fact that while dozens of deliberate murders have been committed in the county since the war, it has had no legal hanging of a murderer. Accordingly, on the morning of March 6, he concealed himself near a spring where his wife went for water for household purposes, and shot her to death when she appeared.

When Mrs. Bright started for the spring just before her death, Bright took his gun and left the house; soon the children heard a shot in the direction of the spring. Bright came back to the house in a few moments and told the children that he had been shot at by some one at the spring. He warned them not to go near the spring, as they might get hurt. The man then filled his pockets with eggs, took his gun and left the house. After a while the children went to the spring and found their mother dead. They gave the alarm and the neighbors gathered in and began the search for the suspected murderer.

He was unable to conceal the crime. He pretended that he had been away in the woods when the deed was done, but his footprints were found where he had stood when he killed her, and a quilt on the brush near the spring had been burned by the flash of his gun. It was apparent that he had stood behind the quilt to shoot her. A brother of the woman, who lived near, refused to believe Bright's story, and made the investigation that indicated that Bright had done the deed. He also came to Forsyth and obtained a warrant, and accompanied the Sheriff when Bright was arrested next day. Bright was lodged in the jail here in Forsyth.

On the 12th the preliminary hearing was begun before Justice W.R. Cox, but Bright's attorneys, as a first step in securing delay, asked for a change of venue, which was granted, and the case was taken before Justice W.H. Jones. There was no charge or belief that either Justice would treat the prisoner unfairly, but the efforts to secure delay exasperated the family of the murdered woman and their friends, because it has invariably happened that delays give the community here time to change their sympathy for the murdered one to the prisoner lying in peril of his life. Then acquittal or inadequate punishment follows.

Two witnesses were heard by Justice Jones and then the case was adjourned until the next day. Deputy Sheriff George L. Williams took the prisoner back to jail. He knew that the woman's relatives were dissatisfied and that a lynching impended, and he was in consequence alert to protect the prisoner. He said during the evening that Lawyers Taylor and McConkey, of the prosecution, had determined to have Bright lynched. He added, "But I'll bluff them if they try it."

At 10 o'clock that night he tried the bluff, but the Ozark mob needs something more. Hearing the mob coming Williams ran from the Hilsabeck Hotel to the jail and, revolver in hand, placed himself before the door. The mob yelled and ordered him away on pain of death for refusal. For a reply Williams said he would shoot the first man who tried to force the door, and, to show that he was armed, fired one shot over the heads of the mob.

The mob had come to the jail that they might adequately, if unlawfully, punish a man for the crime of murder. They found a lawful officer in their way. He was there performing his duty as he had sworn to do, but they deliberately murdered him in order that they might get at and punish another man for murder. As soon as Williams fired, some one in the crowd returned the fire. The Ozark mountaineers are the best kind of marksmen. Williams fell dead with a bullet through his heart. The jail is a little old plank concern, with wooden doors secured by padlocks put through staples. A few blows of a pick opened the way, and Bright was dragged out, carried to a tree, and hanged.

It should be said also that nearly every man in that mob honestly believed he was justified in what he did. A number—perhaps half of them—were church members. Three-fourths of the members of this community belong to some church. In no part of the country are more public discussions over doctrinal points of religion held than in Taney county.

The editor of a newspaper in the adjoining [Christian] county, who knows the people here well, for he lived here once, says, "But why single out Taney county? It is no worse than some other counties in this State in crime, and does not deserve the stigma that is thrust upon it."

That is the way people feel here. They are indignant that people elsewhere should call the county lawless because a murder or a lynching occurs on an average about once in six months.

Sheriff Cook, fearing further lawlessness, telegraphed to Gov. Francis, who replied that the State militia would be sent if needed to arrest members of the mob and preserve order. But nothing has come of it. Both Williams and Bright have been buried, matter is ended. No one will be punished for killing the officer.

## 23
# ACCOMPLICE BETRAYS SECRETS

May 19, 1892.—The betrayal of Dave Walker and his band of Christian county by Joe Inman and Charlie Graves after the Eden-Green massacre, in March, 1887, has a most remarkable parallel in the confession which was made a few days ago in the Springfield jail respecting the murder of Deputy Sheriff Williams and his prisoner, Bright. One of the Taney county mob told the whole story of that double tragedy which for two months some of the Forsyth authorities backed by the assistance of Gov. Francis sought in vain to unveil. The name of the traitor murderer who has given away the secrets of the mob the authorities are withholding yet, but the story is substantially as follows:

> *On Saturday, March 12 last, the day of the preliminary trial of John Wesley Bright, the wife murderer, many of the people from Roark, the scene of the shocking crime, were in Forsyth as witnesses against the uxorcide. George L. Taylor, the young lawyer who had already distinguished himself in the sensational history of Taney county, was busy during the day firing up the mob, especially among the relatives and neighbors of Mrs. Bright. He had gone to Forsyth from Springfield the day before, arriving on the scene about 8 o'clock the previous night. The Forsyth saloon was patronized freely by the organizer of the lynching party during the day. Capt. Mat Day, the old coroner of Taney county, was also active in abetting Taylors' efforts to work up the mob. One by one the vigilant were enrolled until about twenty-three men pledged themselves to help hang Bright. Taylor borrowed a horse of James A.*

*Delaney, attorney of Taney county and stepson of the deceased Bald Knobber chieftain, Capt. [Nat N. Kinney], and rode up Swan creek in the afternoon to engage the services of some men not in town. A place of meeting was selected about a mile north of Forsyth in the Swan creek bottom.*

*Here, about dusk, the lynchers began to assemble. When about fifteen men had gathered in the lonely bottom, Capt. Mat Day, the old hunter, farmer and miller, administered the oath of secrecy and fealty to the band. He was selected to perform this ceremony because, as a charter member of the organization, the ex-coroner knew well all the dread penalties attached to a violation of that solemn obligation. When the oath was administered each man pledged his life and every cent of property he possessed in defense of any member who might be arrested for the crime under contemplation. The mob then moved down the creek toward Forsyth, and other men came and were sworn in by Capt Day. One fellow became scared as he saw the plot thicken, and dodged into the woods and fled. Taylor swore vengeance against the coward, and threatened to shoot down any man who wavered. The killing was talked of and several members of the mob stoutly protested against this suggestion. Then George L. Taylor, Mat Day, Ike Lewis, ex-County Assessor Bill Stockstill and two of his brothers and the three Weatherman boys went aside and held a short consultation.*

What was said by these nine men, the confessing member of the mob could not hear. When the nine leading spirits of the mob came back to their confederates some one asked about the fate of Williams. George Taylor replied, "That's all fixed. If Williams interferes, he will be taken care of."

Then Taylor and Bill Stockstill changed hats and the latter tied a handkerchief over his face, being the only man in the crowd who was disguised. Bill Stockstill had been made captain of the mob. When the crowd crossed the Swan creek ford, about a quarter of a mile from the jail, they gave a yell, put spurs to their horses and galloped into town. Eight or ten confederates were in town watching the officers, and one of these, said to be D.F. McConkey, Taylor's partner, had taken a sledge-hammer from a blacksmith shop and placed it at the jail door. The mob surrounded the jail just as Deputy Sheriff Williams ran up to defend Bright. George Taylor, Bill Stockstill and George Friend were immediately in front of the Deputy Sheriff. Williams raised Taylor's hat with his left hand and said, "George Taylor, I have you spotted."

Immediately Bill Stockstill shot the deputy through the heart. As Williams turned toward the assassin Stockstill fired a second shot. Then Taylor raised the sledge-hammer and began to batter down the door. He soon grew tired and gave the hammer to Bill Stockstill, who hit a few licks and then Ike Lewis took the sledge and completed the work. Taylor went into the jail and tied the rope around Bright's neck, and Bill Stockstill helped drag the prisoner out. Bright was put on a horse behind George Friend and taken about a mile from the jail, where a tree had been selected as a gallows for the victim. Bill Stockstill pulled Bright off the horse and asked him if he had anything to say. The prisoner declined to confess his crime, and was swung up in a few seconds. The mob then dispersed, and Taylor and Bill Stockstill went back to town and joined the crowd that had gathered around the body of the murdered officer.

Stockstill was one of the men who kept vigil that night over the corpse of the man he had shot. These are some of the facts which the state will prove by one of the prisoners held for the murder of Williams and Bright. The eight prisoners confined in the Springfield jail were taken before Justice Chin to-day and released from the charge of murder named in the warrants issued in Greene county. In a moment they were all arrested by Sheriff Day on warrants issued by Justice Jones of Forsyth, who acted as coroner at the inquest held over the bodies of Williams and Bright. This disposes of the habeas corpus.

## 24

# TRAGEDY ENDS IN A FARCE

July 23, 1892.—All the Taney county lynchers who shot and killed Deputy Sheriff George L. Williams and hanged John Wesley Bright, his insane prisoner, at Forsythe on March 11 last are now free.

In the circuit court of Taney county at Forsyth the cases of the twelve men were called and Judge Hubbard over-ruled the motion of the state for a continuance, whereupon Prosecuting Attorney J.L. Davis and C.B. Sharp, his assistant, entered nolle prosequis and the prisoners, who have been in jail since their arrest last May were set at liberty.

It is said that this action was on account of the fact that the State could not get its witnesses and that the court, sheriff and twenty-four of the forty men summoned from which the jury was to be selected were all former members of the Bald Knobbers' organization of Taney county and in sympathy with defendants so that it was impossible to secure a conviction under existing circumstances.

It is also reported that the prosecution will, after the next election when a new judge is on the bench and another sheriff has been elected by the people, secure the reindictment of all the accused and convict them of the crime with which they are charged. One of the officers said that the state had plenty of evidence to convict all the men just as soon as the witnesses could be gotten into court to testify.

*Part III*

# LIFE IN THE OZARKS

# 1

# A BALD KNOBBER'S CABIN

March 24, 1887.—With a Winchester over his shoulder a revolver handy in his pocket, the guide who takes the stranger from Chadwick out over the Ozark Hills, feels happy and secure. In explanation of this display of arms, he says:

> *You see, I've been 'posed to these Bald Knobbers right from the jump, an' o' course they don't like me a gol dang bit. 'Sides, I might git sight o' a deer or something, an' git a pop at him.*

It doesn't make much difference which way one starts, the country is all the same—ridge piled upon ridge, and gap running into gap in the most bewildering manner to any one but a Bald Knobber, or a native of better standing and habits. The stones which cover the hillsides are small, and they roll under the feet and cut into the shoes, so that a walk of a half hour will put a pair of shoes in worse shape than six months tramping in a city. When one experiences this it is easy to understand the extravagant deformity of the shoes on the feet of the Chadwickians. On the ridge the sun strikes warm, but along in the gaps the wind blows unceasingly as if there away off in the mountains somewhere a cave of the winds which was never closed. Looking off from any ridge to the distance on any side of it appears that there are vast sheets of blue water among the trees, but as one advances the water is found to be nothing but smoke from brush fires which are sweeping over the hills, and write strange glowing figures on the slopes at night.

There seems always to be thicker woods on the hills beyond, but reaching them, the marks of a tie-cutters progress is there, and the dead trees, and the dry grass and leaves and the hard flinty rocks make a desolate scene.

## Christian County Eagle

Up against the clear sky there are a few birds wheeling gracefully about with never a flap of wing, and swooping in ravishing curves almost to the ground, up again and away, up till they are absorbed in the blue. These are eagles, and you tell the guide so, with just the vaguest suspicion that you may be away off:

> *Naw, them ain't no eagles; them's buzzards, an' they're wheein' roun' a dead hog down there. They've done been lit an' had dinner.*

The guide punishes the city man's ignorance by starting off at a gait which taxes the lungs and legs to the uttermost. But he softens after awhile, and becomes communicative.

> *Sence the railroad kem in here all the game's got back to the woods, and you can't put a gun top your face. The deer use to stalk right about here—you ken see the lick right over there now.—"Buzzards"—and he laughed to himself—"buzzards ain't no game, an' thy'll fine you $20 mebbe if you shoot'em.*

The nearest house to Chadwick in any direction is fully two miles away, though the view is so clear that one would think he could talk over the gap to the woman sunning herself in the door of the little log cabin, which looks like it had been landed in the hill by a cyclone, and was waiting for it to come back and take it somewhere else. There isn't another house in sight, and the wonder is that people so segregated could organize a body so strong and so swift moving as the Bald Knobbers. But people who live two miles apart in this country are nearer neighbors than people living up and down stairs in the city, and there are few families here in the Ozark Mountains, these haunts of the Missouri kuklux, which are not related either by blood or marriage to every other family. It is the condition of affairs which cause mountains to be deserted now, for the male members of this great mountaineer family who are not in jail are hiding somewhere in the caves in the valleys. Not every resident of these mountains is a Bald Knobber, but a majority of them were at one time, for to be a Bald Knobber once in this country was [to be] greater than a king. None of them are now, if you take their friends' word[s] for it, but the guide who use[d] to be one himself, says:

> *There's mighty few what wasn't in it some time. 'Ef you see a fine farm, which I'm not afeerd you will, you kin bet that don't belong to no Bald Knobber, or a nice house neither. Them belongs to them as was licked an' beat an' to leave the country.*

## A Bald Knobber's Home

The homes of Bald Knobbers are just what would be expected after a look at the barren hills and gloomy gaps, though hardly what would be expected to exist within eighteen hours ride of St. Louis. The primitive nature of their homes can hardly be understood when seen within three or four miles from the railroad station. Progress has a hard fight in this country, and Bald Knobbing is the last obstacle raised to impede the spread of complete civilization in the Southwest. Here in the country, the country which is synonymous with roomies and freedom, it is rather staggering to come upon homes which rival in many disagreeable features the crowded apartments in the big city tenements, whence the young are turned out into the street to develop into thugs and thieves and worse. Where squat right is almost as good as the right to purchase, where the land is open to occupation, there are families of eight and ten, and even twelve, huddled together in one little cabin, and they don't scruple to add a boarder to this if one happens to be passing on the mountain. It is men who live in these hovels who have been masked riders over these hills the last three years regulating the community in their own rude fashion, but are too lazy to add an additional room to their miserable huts as the family increases with rabbit like rapidity. An outside view of a Bald Knobber's home, as seen here and there dotting the hills in this country, is not a cheery one. It is not calculated to make one believe that men who live in such houses would be safe administrators of the law, but it is calculated to aid one in accounting for the existence of masked mobs of murderous night riders, samples of which are now in jail in Springfield and Ozark.

On the side of a hill, or mountain as the hills [are] called, the bottom of the valley behind some ridge which juts out further than others; all about, undistinguishable in color from the general tone of the hills and earth and sky, are these homes. A log cabin sometimes with boards nailed over the spaces between, more often with plastered over with mud, with board roof, a wooden chimney, smeared outside and in with mud; this is the castle of the night-riding Bald Knobber. This invariably contains one room, about ten feet by twelve, or maybe as much as fifteen feet. The apex of the triangular roof is scarcely a dozen feet from the ground, and a moderately grown boy has to stoop to enter the door lest he should split his brains by bumping his head at the top of the jamb. Never a window in this home. Even the sunlight has to stoop down and crouch and crawl into this home. What may not be expected from a home into which the blessed sunlight has to creep like a thief?

## All Pervading Pork

Within this house it takes a stranger some time to become accustomed to the darkness, and when he does he catches a view of an interior such as can be seen seldom anywhere. The smoke from the fireplace, where a log as big as a man's body, lies crackling, has risen to the roof and clung there in soot so that a loud word may jar the boards and cause it to come dropping down flakes. There is a bed of oak, and a table, and a trunk in the corner, which trunk is of old pattern. There are clothes on the wall, and there are hams and shoulders and fletches of bacon hanging along side.

The odor of life, that odor of crowded rooms is prevalent, and then there is the odor of clothes, and the smell of jeans is distinguishable. But over all there is an overpowering odor of pork, and you feel at once that it is the cave of pork-laden zephyrs which sweep over the mountains. Pork! Omnipresent pork. You smell it everywhere, eat it, see it ambling playfully and rooting industriously on the hillsides, hear it squeaking and grunting under the brush in the valleys. It is all prevailing in the Ozarks.

The eye ranging along the wall for a picture, halts rejoiced. Here at last is the evidence of something ideal, something creative. It is a picture, and something Ruskin says about pictures floats dimly through the mind. The picture turns out to be "Sorrel Joe," whose pedigree and valuable services to the country are spoken of very eulogistically below in large, black type.

## Sorrel Joe

Other ornaments were on the wall—a Winchester, a couple shotguns, a belt and holster with a pistol in it, and maybe a deer-knife. In the corner something bright gleams in the darkness, it is a two-edged tie-cutter's ax, the tool before which the old oaks around have fallen and are falling by the hundreds, and the flashings of—which are the will-o-the-wisps which the railroads follow down here into the depths of this wild, rough country. Here are a couple chairs and a cupboard, the door of which stands open and discloses a few cracked cups and a few glasses. There may be occasionally a clock on the cupboard. The miscellany which can not be described take up more room, and, indeed, it is with the greatest care that a stranger must turn around in this home. Here lives a man, his wife and five or six children. There is a small bed under the larger one, which is pulled out for the children to sleep on, but there is no such thing as a screen between them, and disrobing occurs right in one room. Such families as this in cities receive the attention of the police and the sanitary authorities, but it is seldom that an officer, until present Sheriff, Mr. Johnson, was chosen, even venture in this country. The cooking is done in this room where the inmates sleep and the smoke that generates in this process lingers everlastingly up near the roof and in the corners. The wind comes into the house through the chinks in the plaster between logs, and the rain drips through the roof. The dog of the family often sleeps in under the beds on which the family often sleeps. So in a crowded apartment that would be noticeable even if occupied by one man in a city, here in the country, where there is any quantity of space, a half dozen people or more live and enjoy themselves.

## The Lady of the House

It was at a house similar in exterior appearance and internal fullness to the one described that the guide and the *Globe-Democrat* man stopped to rest awhile on their journey over the hills. The man of the house was not at home. He had not been since the night of the massacre for which so many of these mountaineers are now in jail, and it is supposed he is hiding from the Sheriff. A woman was in, sitting at the fireplace on a low, backless chair, with her hair disarranged and falling down on all sides, giving her a distressed air that was touching. On one side clinging to her dress was a little child evidently just learning to walk, and its face lit up with joy it experienced in putting itself up to a standing position. On the other side was an older child who was playing on the floor with some crumbs of cornbread, while from [a] corner very dark and deep there came the sound of another youngster still older who was thumping the bottom of an old tin pan. The stopping of the strangers at the door barred out what few stray gleams of light got in. The woman rose hurriedly and came to the door, and planted herself in it as a barrier to prevent ingress. Her eyes were red and the tears in them had been smeared over the greasy and grimy cheeks with a grimy apron, not enhancing her little beauty, but giving her a kind of tigress look, which lost nothing because in her hasty attempt to arrange her hair she disarrayed it more, and it fell down on her shoulders in an iron gray shower and was dashed about by the wind. She thought evidently the visitors had come to arrest some one, but finding that they were only taking a trip across country, her look mollified considerably, and she passed smoothly and gracefully enough over the conversational commonplaces as to the weather and the strangeness of the country to one unused to it. Then the talk drifted to the all-absorbing topic, the Bald Knobbers:

"How'll it be with them as's bin captured? Pretty hard, I 'spose."

From her tone it was clear, as the guide indicated, she had friends among the captured.

"With some of 'em, mebbe," replied the guide.

"Well, my old man wasn't out no night but onc't since month 'fore last, 'n then he went till the dance down to Swanville, 'n he hain't done nothing. I'm clean sure. W'y he wouldn't hurt—"

She looked around for something capable of being injured, failing to find which, she snapped her finger and finish with: "That!"

There being no contradiction of her assertion, she proceeded:

> But them men ain't goin' to get no jestis up Springfield way. Them 'ere homesteaders comin' down yereabouts just want to run out us old settlers as's lived yere for years, 'n's homes' 'n bin a-grown' of us up jes' like them 'ere trees. Ef'er's bin murder done, 'twzn't done by God-fearin' people, 'n them Sherriffs 'n people'e jes' token off Bapsise 'n Christianses, 'n even poo' Parson Simmons, 's wuz's powful a preacher's ever wuz heard yereabouts.

Life in the Ozarks

## Antique Attitudes

Her feelings rising higher, while the youngest began to cry because he couldn't find anything in the cupboard to catch hold of and raise himself to his feet, she picked him up and began walking up and down the room talking baby-talk to him, and ignoring the visitors so completely that they left her alone with her love and sorrow, and wended their way along the rocky trail still further into the heart of the Swan Creek country. Few men indeed one meets trampling over the hills, for those who are not hiding from the Sherriff are off cutting ties to the south. The women folks and children are in the dark little cabins, and do not come out until long after the stranger has passed, and then they view them with one hand arched over the eye and the other clasping the hip, so that the observer will readily perceive the strength of the claim that the ancients modeled their vases and pitchers on the female form divine; for the akimbo arm makes a perfect handle to the pitcher, outlined against the rocky hill or gray blue spaces between the trees. The traveler's feet may devour the plain, and the eye, be it never so active, it takes in of ten miles but modifications of the view in but one or two miles. There is hill and slope, rising and falling, bare trees and blue sky and pale-blue smoke in the distance, and except the trickling of the spring down the rocky ridge sides, the rustling leaves, the cawing of a crow away off invisible, there is nothing to relieve the ear tortured by the sound of the crunching stone along the paths.

Along the road wagons may be discerned drawn by scrawny ponies, for there are no horses in the mountains, and their progress is slow. The wagons are laden with ties. The railroad tie is the only real product of this country. Gigantic stumps all over the hills mark the tie-cutter's course. Over Chadwick Height a hundred thousand bright new ties can be seen piled along the railroad track. Tie-cutters have mined the woods, and they have marched on to clean the south fifteen miles, where all the day can be heard the ringing music of the axes on the trees, their crash as they fall and the chipping of the axes which are seen flashing in the sun. From Ozark down to Chadwick the hills and valleys have been practically cleared for five miles on either side, and the game has been driven back into the woods. Five miles inland are the deerlicks, and there the huntsmen go for squirrel and turkey and other game, for there—as the guide puts it, "There isn't a stick amiss 'cept those's was struck by lightnin'."

## The Tie-Cutters' Course

Along the line of the railroad are many ruined cabins. They were once the tie-cutter's homes, as described above, but they went on and on as the woods gave way before them. They build homes near the camps, and leave them as the camps are deserted, and in their onward march full many drop the ax forever and lie down to sleep under the rocks and grass in the shady hollows, or on tops of the sun-bathed hills. The tie-cutters make ties at ten cents apiece, and ten ties a day is a good working man's average. If they work for six days in a week they'll average $6.

When they have worked a few days they take a rest, and either shoulder their guns and go hunting or else go visiting. When the food is gone they go to the commissary store, have more food advanced, and then another day off. So the years go around. The houses are very often destitute of food. Indeed, at no times does this class of people fare well, for they are improvident and careless. The grudging earth here in this Bald Knob country gives little for laborious coaxing and gives less for neglect. Before these tie-cutters' homes there may sometimes be a corn patch, but it is a very small patch, indeed. On it there grows just enough corn to keep them in corn meal a year. No man is so poor in this country but what he can own a pig or two, and this much-maligned animal furnishes the greater part of flesh food. The wild onion, the lettuce and potato are the only vegetables as a general rule. A possum, a turkey, a squirrel, or such as fall before the cutter's aim, for no one is so poor here that he a gun of some kind. The women dig seneca root and ginseng with little hoes made for the purpose, and when they have secured a goodly supply they tramp into Chadwick with it, or up to Sparta, and sell it to representatives of the drug trade, in which these roots are very much used. This money from the sale of the root is more often than not invested in canned delicacies, and the cans may be found in the wildest parts near the springs where they serve the very useful purpose of cups.

## The Better Side

This will give you some idea of the poverty of these people, and yet this country [on either side contains] farms [as fine as in any country, and it] is said corn grows abundantly. Up near Ozark there are splendid orchards. Down here, where Bald Knobbers are, there [are] some fine houses, some nice farms, but these do not belong to the men who have been sleeping o' days and riding o' nights, neglecting their own affairs in the regulation of wrongs against the community. When the Bald Knob craze struck the country many of the best men in the country joined the order, but when such men as Ranz Bean, the local desperado, now in the Penitentiary, rose to the divinity of a shining light, most of them dropped out. The men in this Ozark Mountain country, this district about Chadwick, appear to be lazy. The country in days gone by was a good one for an easy woodman's life. They could shoot deer and mink and "sand" the hides and sell them; they could easily raise corn for bread; they had game in abundance; but now the advancing railroad has done away with this. They are not equal to the change, and the shiftless, indecisive, inactive, basking, when their bellies are full, in the sun, chewing tobacco or shooting for a dollar at a marked tree. The old poetic woodland life is gone and the men who live it are dazed by the encroaching of the new life or railroads.

## The Yeoman of Today

The sturdy yeoman who don't do anything but poetically dally among big trees speak lovingly of nature and all that sort of thing, stands revealed to-day as an unkempt, shaggy, down-at-the-heels and out-at-the-toes tobacco-chewing lout.

The bold mountaineer is not visible. The men in this country are long, and lean, and lank unusually. As a general thing they are long-haired as they are long-legged. When seen walking on the hills and contrasted with their little cramped houses, the wonder is how these latter can accommodate the former unless, as their shapes would indicate, they double up like jack-knives when they repose. Some of them must certainly sleep with their feet out of doors. The crouching in the little houses has given them a stoop which adds the impression of their height. Their skins vary between about the color of the black coffee they drink and the iron stains on the rocks in the mountain roads. Some there are so hairy that it is impossible to tell where scalp leaves off and beard begins, or vice versa, and their clothing is generally patched to such extent that the patches have completely taken the place of the original material, and a man thinks he's wearing an entirely new pair of very variegated color, pattern and texture. The patches overlap each other like geologic strata, but has not been estimated, the age of these clothes can't be approximated nearly as close as the age of these everlasting hills. The native is so use[d] to crowding up at home that he crowds his ribs in with his arms in the open air as if he [were] afraid of expansion, and hurries his hands away down in his pockets. Fatness, which in other sections is regarded as one of circumstances over which we have no control, appears to be personally offensive to these people. At least, that's the only objection the Bald Knobbers ever had to the late landlord of Chadwick House, whose obesity, while not aldermanic, was roughly commented upon and termed very objectionable. Most of these men are poor, as shown, and ignorant, and the schoolmaster, though he is abroad now, has not been abroad for long, or else the new Democratic Postmaster at Chadwick wouldn't post in his place of notification that "leters unclad for" will be sent to the "ded leter offis." Books are rare in the Ozark Mountains, though there are three school-houses about this country near Chadwick. The spirit of improvement is slowly getting in its work down here, and the most forcible evidence that it was found to-day when the Chadwick House changed hands, and beef and milk, two luxuries never seen before here, unless in a live state jingling a bell on the hill, appeared on the table. This circumstance was commented on by the old Patriarch of the Ozarks, saying:

> *They be many changes jes now yere-abouts 'n they be more' a' comin. Beef! Swow, I haint eat none cep'n to Ozark or Springfield since long time. Next I spec I'll see the iron horse a snortin 'n a rarin down 'n Taney, 'n then I'll jes give up the battle.*

When the railroad gets to Taney County the millennium will have been reached in the estimation of more people in this country than the Patriarch, and that terra incognita will be opened and the black bears will soon be outnumbered by the voters instead of the reverse, as is now the case.

## 2

# PLUCKY WOMAN SAVED HER HUSBAND

July 8, 1890.—A report comes from across the Arkansas line of a case wherein a band of regulators got decidedly the worst of an attempt to reform one of their neighbors. The old Bald Knobber element which so long dominated this section of the country now remains under the guise of an organization known as Black-Caps. In Arkansas, people take upon themselves the task of reforming all who transgress the moral code but do not stop at this work for they also wreak vengeance upon those who have given members of the band trouble in any way.

    Charles Lawson has been living about eight miles from Newton, in the Ozark range across the state line for the past two years and all those who know him best speak highly of Lawson and his wife. He came to this country with the intention of settling upon government land and selected a piece and entered upon it with the intention of proving up on it as early as possible. He was unfortunate enough to incur the ill will of a member of the band of Black Caps by selecting a piece of timberland that had been occupied by the said member as a squatter. This squatter James Dagget had his full amount of land from the government, but wished to hold the piece of timber for his brother, who was expected to come from Indiana and take up the land. Lawson made his entry, and after a tedious contest, succeeded in getting his patent. During the whole time from the day he first made the claim he has been subjected to petty annoyances and in some instances grievous wrong, but he has born them mildly as he said he wanted no trouble with his neighbors. He and his wife were well liked by all with the exception of the clan that was backing Dagget in his misdeeds.

Mrs. Lawson is a small woman but she is a brave woman and is as nervy as her husband in a fight for a home. On June 28, Lawson received a letter warning him that as he would not leave the country where he was not wanted, when he saw that his neighbors did not like him, he would be given forty-eight hours to get away in, and if he was not gone, then he would have to take the consequences. Lawson was not scared and went about his business.

On the night of the 30$^{th}$ as he was entering his yard having been to town he was suddenly confronted by about ten men wearing black gowns and their heads covered with black caps. He was grasped and tied and the bandits started off to the timber with him. Mrs. Lawson heard the disturbance and quickly divined what was going on. She grasped her husband's Winchester rifle and followed in the dusk until the band with its captive stopped and proceeded to strip the victim preparatory to administering a whipping. Just as the lash was raised to give the first blow a shot rang out and the whipper dropped. In quick succession came two more shots and two more fell while the remainder of the black-caps fled panic stricken as the brave little woman pumped lead after them.

While Mrs. Lawson was cutting her husband's bonds, the last two who fell crawled away in the darkness and escaped, but the whipper lay with a broken thigh. When his black raiment was stripped from him it was found that he was Dagget, and he was sent home by the man who was about to be his victim. When the matter became known, the indignation of the neighbors was so great that they set in to hunt down the band and succeeded in placing five of them in jail, where they now lay awaiting trial.

## 3

# KNOBBER WIVES REFUSE DISCOURAGEMENT

April 11, 1890.—Mrs. C.O. Simmons, wife of the famous Parson Simmons of Bald Knobber distinction, and other women related to the imprisoned regulators are circulating in the eastern part of this county a petition asking Governor Francis to pardon the three convicts confined in the penitentiary for the Edens-Green murders.

The Bald Knobber preacher, in throwing himself on the mercy of the court in a plea of guilty of murder in the second degree, was given twelve years in the penitentiary by Judge Hubbard, while the other two confessing raiders went up for twenty-one years each. As the prisoners have hardly served two years of

David Rowland Francis, Missouri governor, January 14, 1889, to January 9, 1893. *Library of Congress.*

their terms yet it is not probable that the Governor will entertain the prayer for clemency which the women are now circulating. Some friends of the convicts think the present movement premature, but the wives of the Knobbers will not hear any such discouraging suggestions and are getting many names to their petitions.

# 4
# MEET SARAH WALKER

Oct., 1891.—We find this country to be rough broken like most of the southern counties in this State. About eight years ago the Frisco Co. built a branch road from Springfield to Chadwick which is the terminus. Since the building of the R.R. the country has improved very much, which is made apparent on every hand by new farms being opened up, houses and barns built and orchards set out. About all the desirable government land is taken up, though the last official report of the land office at Springfield June the first, '91 showed up 20,000 acres. W.A. Ward, of Fort Smith, is here to locate 80 acres with a land hand warrant which he fell heir to from his grandfather, Wm. Armstrong, who served in the war of 1812; the warrant is dated June 15th, 1836, and it is the first of the kind that has been presented at the land office since 1871, and probably the last one in circulation. Crops are good and prices better than a year ago, consequently business is fair with merchants and traders in general. There has not been any rain here to amount to any thing for three months, hence it is very dry. Forest fires are raging and some of the settlers have lost considerable fencing and some outbuildings and sheds south of here. The acreage of wheat sown is very small owing to the dry weather, and what was sown has only a part come up. Thomas Keen, a gentleman of social qualities and a brother-in-law in of Judge Bland, is here in the produce business. He was a number of years ago a resident of Phelps Co.

We met Sarah Walker, the wife of Dave Walker, the well known Bald Knobber Chief, who was [hanged] at Ozark with his son Wm., about eighteen months ago. She is about 40 years of age, of medium size, with beautiful gray eyes and a massive growth of brown hair which is becoming silvered from worry and trouble that has fell to her to bear. She is the very picture of good nature and friendship, well loved and respected by all. I find people here from a great many States who are all industrious, clever, hospitable, law abiding and well calculated to make many happy homes. We find churches of all denominations and good schools in every district, and as a whole this county is on par with any of the southern counties.

# CONCLUSION

## I'd Been Born Again

As we walk through the seasons of life, we will have many opportunities to be offended and hurt. Our backgrounds might be diverse, our political parties might be varied and our cultures multifaceted. Refusing to care for our neighbor, closing our hearts and disparaging our fellow man will only build and harden the walls of indifference and create our own prison walls, stone by stone. These stones may come handily and are easily thrown.

Deliverance cannot be found in human ingenuity, location or circumstances, but it can be found in the one who created our hearts. When we ask for forgiveness from above and from our neighbors, we have the opportunity to walk exonerated by our Maker, and then we can pardon our fellow man. May we all glean the hope of true life, liberty and the pursuit of happiness.

I leave you with a small chronicle of former Bald Knobber, Reverend C.O. Simmons, when he described his deliverance from the sentence of death. This is recorded from a 1903 article that quotes District Judge N.M. Shelton:

> *Men don't want to die—except in novels. There the hero can afford to be indifferent to danger because he knows that if the right sort of author has hold of him, he will get through somehow and live happy ever after. But ordinary humankind wants to live as long as the blood of life and health flows. There are no two sides to the subject. While a spark of intelligence exists in saint or sinner life is the dearest thing there is. It is the law of nature's God.*

## Conclusion

Newspaper illustration of Reverend C.O. Simmons in the Missouri Penitentiary. *Library of Congress.*

*I was a member of the Missouri senate in 1889. The capital buildings and Penitentiary are at Jefferson City. A Baptist preacher, a Bald Knobber, named Simmons, had been sentenced to death for murder. He was regarded as courageous to the point of recklessness. At the last moment the governor commuted the sentence to imprisonment for life. I saw the old man as he was dressed in the penitentiary. His face glowed with pleasure. Life had come back to him and it was overpoweringly sweet. Someone asked him how he felt. He had nothing to look forward to but grim, incessant toil, under a hard master, through all the years to come. But he would live, and he was profoundly grateful therefore. Simmons responded with a quotation he had doubtless used many a time in the days before he went to the bad:*
    *"Glory to God! I feel just like I'd been born again."*

*Appendix*

# THE BALLAD OF THE BALD KNOBBERS

This ballad is from the Bald Knobber era and was probably written by Anti-Bald Knobbers in the 1880s. Reports attribute its lyrics to Andrew, "Andy," or Robert Coggburn. According to author Vance Randolph's book, *Ozark Folksongs*, Mary Elizabeth Mahnkey, a daughter of an original Bald Knobber, A.S. Prather, testifies to the originality. She also recalls its lyrics to the melody of "My Name is Charles Guiteau."

### THE BALLAD OF THE BALD KNOBBERS

*Adieu to old Kirbyville, I can no longer stay,*
*Hard times and Bald Knobbers has driven me away,*
*Hard times and Bald Knobbers has caused me for to roam,*
*My name is Andrew Coggburn, near Kirbyville's my home.*
*My friends and relations, it's much against my will.*
*To leave my dear old mother and go from Kirbyville.*
*But for the sake of dear ones, who want me for to go,*
*I'll arm myself with weapons and I'm off to Mexico.*

*Bald Knobbers are no gentlemen, they're nothing more than hogs,*
*they tried to hunt me down and treat me like a dog.*
*They're nothing but big rascals, and their names I'll expose.*
*They'll take all of your money and rob you of your clothes.*

# Appendix

*There's one big Bald Knobber who is a noted rogue.*
*He stole from Joseph Bookout some sixteen head of hogs.*
*Walked boldly in the courthouse and swore they was his own.*
*He stole them by the drove and horsed 'em over home.*

*There's another Bald Knobber who rides a pony blue.*
*He robbed old Nell MacCully and Mister Thompson, too.*
*He took from them their money and from them rode away,*
*And now the highway robbers is the big men of the day.*
*There's one big black rascal whose name I will expose.*
*His name is Nat N. Kinney, and he wears his Federal clothes.*
*He tries to boss the people and make them do his will.*
*There's some that does not fear him, but others mind him still*

*To raise Bald Knobber excitement, I made a splendid hand.*
*I don't fear judge nor jury, I don't fear any man.*
*If the Knobbers want to try me, they've nothing else to do.*
*I'll take me my old Colt and I'll make an opening through.*

# Appendix

*These Knobbers run the country, but they can't keep it up.*
*They'll stick their tail between their legs, like any other pup.*
*And there's a day a-coming when they will hunt their dens,*
*And if I'm not mistaken, there's some will find their ends.*

*I've tried to live in peace with all, Bald Knobbers they say no;*
*And if you don't do what they say, you have to up and go.*
*My mother begs and pleads with me, she's fearful for my life;*
*She wants me to depart from here & from Bald Knobber strife.*
*For each stripe that they gave me, I've sworn to get a man,*
*I'm spending all my time now in thinning down the klan.*
*And there's a day a-coming when they all will hunt their dens,*
*And if I'm not mistaken, there's more will find their ends.*

# BIBLIOGRAPHY

*Atchison Daily Globe.* "Grieved in Spirit." March 18, 1887. www.chroniclingamerica.loc.gov (accessed April 20, 2011).

———. "The Tough Lands." July 20, 1889. www.chroniclingamerica.loc.gov (accessed April 20, 2011).

*Cape Girardeau Democrat.* "Betrayed." May 28, 1892. www.chroniclingamerica.loc.gov (accessed April 20, 2011).

———. "In Taney County." March 26, 1892. www.chroniclingamerica.loc.gov (accessed April 20, 2011).

Coggburn, Andrew. "Bald of the Bald Knobber." Circa 1886. Public Domain. Christian County Library (accessed April 20, 2011).

*Daily Alta California.* "Bald Knobbers at War." July 9, 1888. www.cdnc.ucr.edu (accessed March 25, 2012).

———. "Brutal Bald Knobbers." February 26, 1888. www.cdnc.ucr.edu (accessed March 25, 2012).

———. "Whisky Raid in a Missouri Town." November 13, 1886. www.cdnc.ucr.edu (accessed March 25, 2012).

## Bibliography

*Emporia Weekly News*, "Executed." May 16, 1889. www.chroniclingamerica.loc.gov (accessed April 26, 2012).

*Evening Bulletin*. "Three of Noted Gang Hanged at Ozark, Mo." May 11, 1889. www.chroniclingamerica.loc.gov (accessed April 20, 2012).

*Evening World*. "Bald Knobbers' Reign." May 22, 1888. www.chroniclingamerica.loc.gov (accessed April 26, 2012).

*Fort Worth Daily Gazette*. "A Bald Knobber." March 24, 1890. www.chroniclingamerica.loc.gov (accessed April 20, 2012).

———. "County Seat War." March 4, 1890. www.chroniclingamerica.loc.gov (accessed April 20, 2012).

———. "Saved Her Husband." July 9, 1890. www.chroniclingamerica.loc.gov (accessed April 20, 2012).

Galbraith, Frank H. *Galbraith's Railway Mail Service Maps, Missouri*. Chicago, 1898. Library of Congress Geography and Map Division. www.loc.gov (accessed April 20, 2012).

Hartman, Mary, and Elmo Ingenthron. *Bald Knobbers: Vigilantes on the Ozarks Frontier*. 1988. Reprint, Gretna, LA: Pelican Pub. Co., 1988.

*Helena Daily Independent*. "The Cowardly Crime." April 14, 1889. www.chroniclingamerica.loc.gov (accessed April 21, 2012).

———. "Noted Criminals." April 14, 1889. www.chroniclingamerica.loc.gov (accessed April 21, 2012).

*Indian Arrow*. "Wiley Mathews." June 27, 1889. www.gateway.okhistory.org (accessed May 20, 2012).

*Indian Chieftain*. "News of the Week." November 28, 1889. www.gateway.okhistory.org (accessed May 21, 2012).

*Iola Register*. "Lynchers Released." July 29, 1892. www.chroniclingamerica.loc.gov (accessed April 20, 2012).

# Bibliography

*Los Angeles Herald.* "Big Jail Delivery." December 30, 1888. www.cdnc.ucr.edu (accessed March 25, 2012).

*McNally Atlas Map of the United States, 1888.* Jim Bohannon Collection. Donald W. Reynolds Library. Recorded September 10, 2010. compact disc.

*Middlebury Register.* "William Marion Miles." September 14, 1888. www.chroniclingamerica.loc.gov (accessed April 20, 2010).

*Missouri Message.* "Bald Knob Survivor Dies." 1908. www.chroniclingamerica.loc.gov (accessed April 21, 2012).

*Morning Constitution.* "Knobber Wives." April 12, 1890. www.chroniclingamerica.loc.gov (accessed April 21, 2012).

*New-York Tribune.* "Work for the Historian." June 23, 1887. www.chroniclingamerica.loc.gov (accessed April 21, 2010).

*Oklahoma Representative.* "Bald Knobbers Favored." July 2, 1897. www.gateway.okhistory.org (accessed May 21, 2012).

*Oregon Scout.* "Arrests by the Wholesale." March 26, 1887. www.chroniclingamerica.loc.gov (accessed April 21, 2010).

*Red Cloud Chief.* "A Horrible Scene." May 17, 1889. www.gateway.okhistory.org (accessed May 20, 2012).

*Sacramento Daily Union.* "They Are Doing Some Lively Work." March 25, 1890. www.cdnc.ucr.edu (accessed March 25, 2012).

———. "Three of Them Expiate." May 11, 1889. www.cdnc.ucr.edu (accessed March 25, 2012).

*Saint Louis Globe-Democrat.* "Applegate Acquitted." September 7, 1887. ww.newspaperarchive.com (accessed April 22, 2012).

———. "Bald Knobber Chief." July 12, 1887. www.newspaperarchive.com (accessed April 22, 2012).

# Bibliography

———. "Charley Graves Makes a Clean Breast." April 21, 1887. www.newspaperarchive.com (accessed April 22, 2012).

———. "Christian County Regulators Again on Trial at Ozark." August 23, 1887. www.newspaperarchive.com (accessed April 27, 2012).

———. "On the Ozark Hills." March 26, 1887: 3. www.newspaperarchive.com (accessed April 22, 2012).

———. "Trial of Gilbert Applegate." September 2, 1887. www.newspaperarchive.com (accessed April 20, 2012).

*Saint Paul Daily Globe*. "Bald Knobbers." April 24, 1887. www.chroniclingamerica.loc.gov (accessed April 24, 2012).

———. "An Eye for an Eye." August 25, 1888. www.chroniclingamerica.loc.gov (accessed April 24, 2012).

———. "Quintuple Lynching." November 16, 1888. www.chroniclingamerica.loc.gov (accessed April 24, 2012).

———. "Set Free by Friends." December 30, 1888. www.chroniclingamerica.loc.gov (accessed April 24, 2012).

———. "Three Bald Knobbers Strangled to Death at Ozark, Mo." May 11, 1889. www.chroniclingamerica.loc.gov (accessed April 20, 2011).

*Salt Lake Herald*. "In Taney County, Missouri." 7 Aug. 1889. www.chroniclingamerica.loc.gov (accessed April 20, 2012).

———. "Murders Break Jail." December 30, 1888. www.chroniclingamerica.loc.gov (accessed April 20, 2012).

*Sedalia Weekly Bazoo*. "Died at His Post." March 22, 1992. www.chroniclingamerica.loc.gov (accessed April 20, 2012).

*Sun*. "Bald Knobbers." December 23, 1888. www.chroniclingamerica.loc.gov (accessed April 22, 2011).

## Bibliography

———. "Bald Knobbers." December 30, 1888. www.chroniclingamerica.loc.gov (accessed April 22, 2011).

———. "Bald Knobbers Sentenced to Death." March 29, 1888. www.chroniclingamerica.loc.gov (accessed April 22, 2011).

———. "John Matthews Captured." January 2, 1889. www.chroniclingamerica.loc.gov (accessed April 22, 2011).

———. "Ozark Mountain Crime." April 1, 1892. www.chroniclingamerica.loc.gov (accessed April 22, 2011).

———. "Pious Bald Knobbers." April 25, 1886. www.chroniclingamerica.loc.gov (accessed April 22, 2011).

———. "Rescued from the Gallows." December 30, 1888. www.chroniclingamerica.loc.gov (accessed April 22, 2011).

Upton, Lucile M. *Bald Knobbers*. Point Lookout, MO: School of the Ozarks Press, 1939.

Vance Randolph. *Ozark Folksongs*. Chicago: University of Illinois Press, 1982: 175.

*Virginia Enterprise*. "Dread the Gallows." July 17, 1903. www.chroniclingamerica.loc.gov (accessed April 20, 2012).

*Wichita Eagle*. "Bungling Work." May 11, 1889. www.chroniclingamerica.loc.gov (accessed April 27, 2009).

———. "Criminal Calendar." April 22, 1887. www.chroniclingamerica.loc.gov (accessed April 27, 2009).

———. "Hundreds on the Hunt." July 9, 1889. www.chroniclingamerica.loc.gov (accessed April 27, 2009).

———. "Murder Cases Postponed." August 15, 1889. www.chroniclingamerica.loc.gov (accessed April 27, 2009).

## Bibliography

———. "Once More at Large." April 22, 1887. www.chroniclingamerica.loc.gov (accessed April 27, 2009).

———. "Recent Circus." August 11, 1889. www.chroniclingamerica.loc.gov (accessed April 27, 2009).

# INDEX

## A

Abbott, E.T. 114
Abbott, Joseph 114
Abbott, M.V. 114
Abbott, William 91, 114
Adams, Andy 88, 103, 108, 115
Adams, J.N. 87
Adams, T.C. 87
Aggernite, George 8
Anderson, Emmett 7, 125
Applegate, Gilbert 79, 85, 88, 96, 103, 113, 115, 121, 122, 123, 126
Applegate, Mrs. 121
Arkansas 29, 48, 49, 50, 59, 89, 127, 167
Armstrong, Wm. 171

## B

*Baldknobbers Hillbilly Jamboree Stage Show* 7
"Ballad of the Bald Knobbers" 175
Barker, Rufus 65
Barker, Sampson 14, 49
Baxter County, Arkansas 99
Bear Creek 62
Bedford, William 133

Bell, Morgan 114
Berry, J.S.B. 42, 52, 67
Berry, Mrs. A.E. 52, 53, 54, 55, 56, 57, 58, 60
Berry's Hotel 53
Bird, Elder 87
Bland, Judge 171
Blevens, J.H. 114
Blue Ridge 78
Bookout, Joseph 176
Boyd, S.H. 112
Branson, Galba E. 20, 44, 61, 62, 63, 65, 67
Branson, Missouri 7
Bridges, Nancy 121
Bridges, S.R. 112, 115, 122
Bright, John Wesley 147, 150, 153
Bright, Mrs. 147, 150
Brooks, James 128
Brooks, West 44
Brown, James 50, 128
Brown, J.J. 16, 20, 22, 122
Bruton, J.J. 114
Bull Creek 71, 90, 102, 115, 130, 134, 137, 146

# INDEX

## C

Chadwick, Missouri 78, 90, 91, 92, 93, 96, 101, 102, 105, 108, 115, 117, 124, 125, 127, 130, 138, 143, 144, 146, 157, 158, 163, 164, 165, 166, 171
Charles Lawson 168
Cherry Grove School House 69
Chin, Justice 152
Christian County, Missouri 22, 60, 68, 70, 75, 76, 78, 80, 86, 89, 90, 91, 92, 101, 102, 105, 106, 107, 108, 109, 110, 111, 115, 116, 121, 124, 127, 128, 129, 130, 131, 134, 137, 138, 143, 144, 149, 150
Christian County, MIssouri 92
Clements, C.C. 114
Coggburn Andrew 37, 39, 40, 42, 46, 47, 86, 128, 175
Coggburn, Andrew 175
Coggburn, John 37, 41
Coggburn, Robert 175
Collins, James 132, 133
Combs, Arbert 62
Combs family 63
Combs, Westley 65
Company H, Sixteenth Missouri 103, 137
Company M, Sixth Missouri 137
Cook, Sheriff 149
Cowan, D.M. 114
Cox, W.R. 148
Cummings store 62

## D

Dagget, James 167, 168
David, William 108
Davis, J.L. 153
Davis, Lewis 88, 96, 126
Davis, Peter 88
Day, Madison 65
Day, Mat 150, 151
Day, Sheriff 152

Delaney, J.A. 151
DeLong, J.A. 13, 20, 21, 36, 57, 58, 60
Dennis, James H. 62
Dennison, Rev. 42
Dickinson, John T. 28, 29, 44, 128
Dome, Andrew Watson 40
Dorland, George 114
Douglas County, Missouri 75, 78, 80, 89, 93, 127, 131
Droopy Drawers 7

## E

Eddleman, J.F. 114
Eden, James 125
Edens, Elizabeth 83, 114
Edens, James 83, 114, 115, 116, 118, 120, 122, 129
Edens, Will 83, 84
Edens, William 81, 83, 84, 115, 117, 119, 120, 122, 123, 128, 130, 131, 134
Eglinton Cemetery 32
Enders, William 125
Eureka Springs, Arkansas 62
Evans, John 131, 138
Evans, Thomas 114
Evans, Will 82
Everett, J.M. 16, 17, 20, 21, 25, 61, 128
Everett, Rev. 42
Everett, Sam 17
Everett, Yell 16, 18, 20

## F

Fickle, P.F. 20
Finley Township 114
Flood, Joshua 114, 123
Forsyth, Missouri 13, 14, 16, 17, 20, 25, 27, 28, 29, 31, 34, 38, 43, 44, 46, 48, 49, 50, 52, 57, 61, 62, 67, 69, 71, 75, 89, 128, 148, 150, 151, 152, 153
Fort Smith, Arkansas 171
Foster, T.A. 114
Francis, Governor 149, 150

# INDEX

Franklin, Jerry  49
Friend, George  151, 152
Fulbright, J.H.  114
Funk, Ed  61, 62, 63, 65, 66, 67

## G

Garrett, Miranda  28
George Aggernite  7
Gideon, J.J.  103, 112, 122
Gilmore, H.G.  114
Graves, Charles  22, 85, 101, 107, 114, 150
Green, Amanda  114, 116, 119
Green, Charles  83, 84, 85, 86, 88, 90, 94, 115, 116, 117, 118, 120, 123, 125, 128, 130, 131, 134
Green, Deputy Sheriff  112
Greene County, Missouri  26, 45, 108, 127, 137, 152
Greene County, Missouri  75
Green, Elizabeth  114
Green, George  114, 120, 122
Green, Melvina  83, 87, 129

## H

Haislip, Wm.  114
Hale, Judge  114
Hammond, J.A.  122
Hanks, Thos.  114
Harrington, Almus "Babe"  96, 101, 115, 122
Harrison, Arkansas  59
Hartman, Mary  9
Haworth, Reverend  42
Helms, E.P.  104
Henry, Jas.  114
Hensley, William P.  44
Herrell, Newton W.  25
Herrington, "Babe"  55
Hiles, Andrew  90, 114
Hiles, Jack  90, 104, 114
Hill, C.O.  87, 88
Hilsabeck Hotel  55, 148
Hindman, Deputy Sheriff  112

Hinkle, Dan  69
Hodes, John P.  104
Holt, James L.  48, 128
*Home and Farm* newspaper  16
Horn, T.B.  136
Howell County, Missouri  75
Hubbard, Judge  60, 110, 113, 123, 153, 169
Hull, Sam  17
Hunt, William  48
Hyde, Joseph  88, 90, 91, 92

## I

Ingenthron, Elmo  9
Inman, Joseph "Joe"  85, 89, 90, 91, 92, 93, 96, 97, 98, 107, 108, 114, 150
Isaacs, Reuben  44, 65

## J

Jamison, J.C.  44
Johnson, J.S.  114
Johnson, Zachariah  78, 87, 96, 99, 100, 103, 107, 131, 132, 133, 138
Jones, Amos  88, 90, 91, 126
Jones, W.H.  32, 148, 152

## K

Kansas  56, 89
Keen, Thomas  171
Kinney, Nathaniel N.  8, 13, 14, 16, 17, 19, 20, 21, 22, 23, 29, 30, 32, 33, 38, 39, 40, 41, 42, 44, 45, 46, 47, 50, 52, 53, 54, 56, 57, 58, 59, 60, 61, 63, 64, 67, 70, 76, 78, 86, 87, 127, 128, 144, 146, 151, 176
Kintrea's Store  47
Kirbyville, Missouri  47, 55, 61, 63, 64, 65, 68, 175
Kissee, A.C.  27, 44
Kissee, Arter  36

# Index

## L

Lasley, Andrew 121
Lawson, Charles 167
Lawson, John 114
Lawson, Mrs. 168
Layton, Al 17, 19, 25, 48, 62, 69, 128
Layton, Sam 18
Layton, Thomas A. 14, 19, 34, 35, 69
Lead Hill, Arkansas 50
Lee, J.L. 114
Lewis, Ike 151, 152

## M

Mabe, Lyle W. 7
MacCully, Nell 176
Mahnkey, Mary Elizabeth 175
Manus, James 50, 128
Mapes, H.J. 111
Mapes, John 111
Mapes, William 111
Mariey, William 114
Marmaduke, Governor 42, 44
Mathews, James 88, 115
Mathews, Jimmie 138
Mathews, John 82, 86, 88, 91, 94, 95, 99, 102, 109, 115, 126, 130, 132, 133, 134, 135, 136, 137, 138
Mathews, Wiley 82, 84, 88, 91, 94, 115, 126, 130, 133, 134
Mayden, Arch 121
McConkey, D.F. 151
McGuire, James R. 114
McHaffie, J.K. 20, 48
McWilliams, Beck 78
Melton, Ansel 114
Mercer, Buck 36, 42, 128
Middleton, George "Wash" Washington 47, 128
Miles, Jim 63, 65, 66, 68
Miles, William, Jr. 42, 56, 58, 59, 60, 63, 64, 67, 68, 128
Miles, William, Sr. 42
Miller, Deputy 87

Mills, J.H. 114
Mills, W.B. 114
Milum, Price 50
Mincey Valley 48
Mogart, Jesse 114
Mogart, John 114
Moseley, John 14, 19, 34
Mountain Home, Arkansas 7

## N

Nash, John 114
Nash, Mat 114
Neville, Deputy Sheriff 92
Neville, J.H. 93
Newton County, Arkansas 48
Newton, J.D. 138
Newton, Lois 99
Newton, William 88, 90, 91, 99, 103, 115
New York, New York 139
Nix, Thomas 114
Norman, Lois 45
Nubbin Ridge 27, 28, 32, 36, 45, 57, 60

## O

Oak Grove Church 38, 40
Owens 33
Owens, Bill 132
Ozark County, Missouri 7, 75, 89, 127
Ozark, Missouri 7, 16, 27, 40, 42, 44, 49, 55, 59, 70, 87, 88, 92, 94, 96, 97, 106, 107, 108, 110, 112, 123, 124, 127, 131, 132, 133, 135, 144, 148, 149, 157, 158, 159, 163, 164, 165, 166, 171

## P

Parrish, A.L. 32
Parthenon, Arkansas 48
Patterson 16, 20, 128
Phelps County, Missouri 171
Phillips, T.W. 20
Pierce City, Missouri 93

# INDEX

Power 33
Prather, A.S. 20, 33, 44, 56, 175
Preston, James 87, 91, 114
Preston, Sam 83, 87, 91
Price, Ben 16
Pruitt, America 71
Pruitt, Reuben 49, 128
Pruitt, William A. 71, 72

## R

Ralston, J.P. 114, 121
Randolph, Vance 175
Ray, Bud 82, 83, 87
Ray, Larkin 114
Ray, W.J. 114
Reuben, Judge 114
Reynolds, J.J. 34
Reynolds, Judge 43
Rhoades, John 78
Rice, J.B. 20
Ring, Amus 25, 128
Roark 147, 150
Roberts, Bill 83, 87, 90
Robertson, Jesse 104, 114
Robertson, T.L. 114
Rogers, J.C. 114

## S

Sharp, C.B. 153
Shelton, N.M. 173
Shepherd of the Hills 7
Silver Dollar City 7
Simmons 174
Simmons, C.O. 78, 82, 84, 87, 88, 90, 91, 92, 96, 97, 103, 108, 109, 112, 115, 121, 126, 162, 169, 173
Simmons, Houston 114
Sloan 87
Smelter Hollow 83
Smith, W.S. 114
Smyrna Church 112
Snapp, Sam 40, 41, 47, 128
Sparta Cemetery 87

Sparta, Missouri 78, 81, 82, 83, 86, 87, 90, 101, 105, 115, 116, 137, 139, 164
Spears 33
Spellings, T.C. 14, 34, 105
Springfield, Missouri 7, 13, 14, 17, 26, 30, 31, 46, 61, 63, 64, 90, 92, 93, 103, 105, 107, 112, 127, 131, 143, 150, 152, 159, 162, 166, 171
Stanley, William 88, 109, 111, 115, 126
Stewart, Nelson 114
St. John, Richard 114
St. Louis and San Francisco Railroad 143
St. Louis, Missouri 14, 143, 159
Stockstill, Austin 62, 151, 152
Stockstill, Bill 151, 152
Stockstill family 63
Stone County, Missouri 75
Sublett, Elijah 29
*Sun* newspaper 23
Swan Creek 83, 106, 108, 143, 151, 163
Swearingin, Bill 78
Swearingin, Dodge 78, 79
Swearingin, George 78
Swearingin, Levi 79
Swearingin settlement 78

## T

Taney City, Missouri 60, 140, 141
Taney County, Missouri 9, 13, 14, 16, 21, 26, 27, 33, 34, 35, 37, 38, 39, 42, 43, 44, 45, 46, 49, 50, 53, 54, 60, 61, 62, 65, 66, 69, 70, 78, 80, 89, 93, 98, 127, 128, 129, 130, 133, 140, 141, 142, 143, 146, 147, 149, 150, 151, 153, 166
*Taney County News* 13
Taylor, Frank 27, 28, 29, 31, 32, 44, 45, 128
Taylor, George L. 49, 53, 128, 150, 151
Taylor, Tubal 27, 28, 29, 32, 33, 44, 45, 128

Taylor, William  44, 45, 46, 128
Texas  60, 89
Toney, T.H.  30, 32
Travers, O.H.  103, 112
Turner, Samuel  114

# V

VanZandt  33
VanZandt, J.R.  20, 23

# W

Walker, David  78, 80, 82, 84, 85, 86,
    88, 90, 91, 99, 103, 105, 110,
    115, 124, 125, 126, 130, 131,
    134, 137, 144, 145, 146, 150, 171
Walker, John  99
Walker, Sarah  171
Walker, William  82, 84, 85, 86, 87, 88,
    98, 99, 100, 108, 115, 126, 130,
    134, 135, 136, 137, 138
Wallace, Tillman  114
Ward, W.A.  171
Warren, George  69, 128
Watson, G.A.  87, 101
Weatherman boys  151
White River  25, 60, 143, 144, 147
Wiley, Jonathan  125
Williams, George L.  148, 149, 150,
    151, 152, 153
Wilson, Ames  124
Wilson, John  112
Winkle  33
Wolf, F.M.  103, 112

# Y

Yeasy, Liash  30

# ABOUT THE AUTHOR

Vincent S. Anderson is a native of the Ozarks and a veteran of the U.S. Air Force. He has bachelor's degrees in biblical studies and mid-level education. Vincent currently works as a historic librarian and lectures on Ozarks history. He serves on the board of directors for the Arkansas Genealogical Society and has worked as a historic consultant for the Travel Channel and the SyFy Channel. He has authored historical articles for newspapers, quarterlies and his website, Ozarks History. He was raised in Ozark County, Missouri, and currently lives in Baxter County, Arkansas.

*Visit us at*
www.historypress.net

This title is also available as an e-book

www.ingramcontent.com/pod-product-compliance
Lightning Source LLC
Chambersburg PA
CBHW042142160426
43201CB00022B/2374